JEANNE CALMENT, THE SECRET OF LONGEVITY UNRAVELLED

Volume I

The switch

Nikolay Zak and Philip Gibbs

CONTENTS

PREFACE

Seek not the favor of the multitude; it is seldom got by honest and lawful means. But seek the testimony of few; and number not voices, but weigh them.

Immanuel Kant

In 2018-2019 evidence emerged that Jeanne Calment's outlying record longevity claim could be invalid. According to an old hypothesis revitalised by Nikolay Zak, Mme Calment who died in 1997 with a validated age of 122 years and 164 days, was in fact Jeanne Calment's daughter Yvonne who had masqueraded as her mother since 1934 when Yvonne was reported to have died.

The hypothesis was supported by circumstantial evidence including clear inconsistencies in Mme Calment's celebrated claim to have met Van Gogh and her testimony that she was escorted to school by a maid Marthe Fousson that records show could only be true for Yvonne.

Four years on we investigate the case with the addition

of new finds that strengthen the reasons to believe in the identity switch. This includes new examples of signatures that show a dramatic change of Jeanne's autograph from the year before her daughter's death, and testimony from the family of Dr. Gilbert indicating that it was Jeanne who was ill with tuberculosis in 1931 rather than Yvonne.

In January 2022 INSERM released digital copies of 15 hours of audio recordings of interviews with Jeanne Calment from 1992 to 1996 that were used by her validation team to confirm her authenticity. We have analysed these tapes and find numerous examples of identity slips and inconsistencies ignored by the validators in their books.

The original interviews show that the revalidation of Calment's record performed by her supporters in 2019 was partially based on inaccurate representation of what she said.

In this trilogy we untangle the biographies of Jeanne and Yvonne, presenting an exhaustive study of their lives and subsequent controversy and investigations. We contend that our new evidence provides overwhelming support for the identity switch hypothesis. We also refute counterclaims made by the original validators and their supporters.

Jeanne Calment's longevity is a key demographic data point frequently cited in the gerontology literature. It has influenced projections of future life expectancy and could have helped shape retirement age policy in Europe. We call on French authorities to instigate DNA tests that would definitively settle the scientifically important question of her longevity.

We argue that her case is still exceptionally interesting because it demonstrates how easily a small lie can grow, spread, and become universally accepted. This extraordinary story should be studied, but it belongs to the field of human psychology, not gerontology.

WHY IS IT
IMPORTANT

*Madame Calment has exceeded the mythical limit of
120 years, beyond which there are no more limits...
The thousands of centenarians who are following in her
footsteps show us that the extension of life span affects
everyone. She was not a mutant but a precursor.*

M. Allard and J.-M. Robine [1]

In the beginning of this century demographers
discovered what they have called *"the most remarkable
regularity of the mass endeavour ever observed"*:

*Human life expectancy in the record-holding
country had risen for more than 150 years at a
steady pace of almost 3 months per year.* [2]

But how long can this trend last? To determine the
answer, experts in aging have been locked in a debate as
to whether the mortality rates continue to rise in late life,

or reach a plateau? As demographer Jean-Marie Robine explained

"If there is a mortality plateau, then there is no limit to human longevity." [3]

In 1990s Robine discovered a clue suggesting that the plateau does indeed exist. He led the team that validated the longevity of the living record holder Jeanne Calment and found her age of over 120 years to be authentic [4].

Even though such exotic ages are not included in the mortality tables and do not directly affect the calculations of annuity and pension providers, the impact of this longevity validation has been surprisingly far reaching.

Encouraged by the experimental confirmation for the theory of a mortality plateau provided by Calment, Robine and James Vaupel, the founding director of the Max Planck Institute for Demographic Research, inaugurated the International Database on Longevity (IDL).

The database containing validated lifespans of *supercentenarians* (those older than 110 years) allowed their team to develop the mathematics which indicates that

"The annual risk of death after age 114 cannot rise much above 50% unless Jeanne Louise Calment's rigorously documented lifespan of 122.45 years is fraudulent." [5]

After verification of Calment's record, Robine and his colleagues forecast a huge forthcoming wave of supercentenarians. Vaupel had also made a bold prediction that

> *"Half of the girls and a third of the boys recently born in the developed world will live to be 100."* [6]

In 2011 Vaupel improved this forecast suggesting that

> *"Most children born since the year 2000 will live to see their 100th birthdays in the 22nd century."* [7]

He elaborated the mainstream view on the demography of ageing in the address to the Global forum for Longevity organized by the French multinational insurance company AXA:

> *"In the foreseeable future, no slowing in the trend is projected and there is no empirical proof or theoretical reason to support a halt in the rise. Perhaps there exists a limit to lifespan—150, 200 or an age that we cannot even imagine.*
>
> *Jeanne Calment (the Frenchwoman who for the moment is humanity's longest living individual) died at the age of 122. Therefore, we have no visibility beyond 122 years. Perhaps something happens at that age, but as far as we know, there is not any insurmountable barrier."* [8]

The models for future mortality proposed by Vaupel

are used by governments and insurance companies to evaluate the pension policy and annuity payments [9]. In 2018 he voiced support for the Netherlands' decision to raise the retirement age for the state pension and claimed it was more likely that life expectancy would increase spectacularly than that it was to stabilise [10].

In the scientific literature, the controversial view that longevity can continue to grow at a steady pace was often justified by the age of Jeanne Calment and other, often dubious, extreme age claims [11]. Nevertheless, the debate is not yet over, as the other side continues to argue for limits on maximum and average life expectancy [12].

In the UK the retirement age is set to rise from 65 to 68, and in France, from 62 to 67, subject to political change: there have been calls to delay this increase because human longevity has not increased in-line with expectations over the last decade [13].

The lengthening of working life is a highly unpopular measure affecting the poor much more heavily than the wealthy. Not only can the rich afford to retire early on their own funds, but they also enjoy a life expectancy as much as 9 years higher than the least well-off [14, 15, 16].

Any decision to go ahead with such measures should depend on future projection of human life expectancy. The models currently in use have been shaped by the belief that there are no biological barriers to increased longevity which was reinforced by Calment's astonishing record.

Since his work on validating the record of human longevity, Jean-Marie Robine has become an influential demographer: the number of references to his publications has increased some 300-fold. In an interview for Le Monde a few days before the French presidential election of 2022 he advocated for application of his Healthy Life Expectancy Indicator, the EVSI:

> *"If we want a just society, if we cannot act on death or illness, we can at least act on the retirement age."* [17]

There is a certain irony that the claimed longevity of Mme Calment who had never worked was used to justify the increase of pensionable age. It is important that policies are based on sound data. Calment's validation is commonly referred to as the gold standard of age verification, but how fair is this high praise?

Even while Calment was alive, Nicolas Brouard, research director at France's National Demographics studies Institute (INED), showed her validators a calculation employing a model without a mortality plateau which if correct would force them to conclude that Jeanne's daughter Yvonne had assumed her identity. This was published by Robine's co-validator Michel Allard on his (now defunct) website dedicated to the supercentenarian [18].

There were only two possibilities. Either Jeanne Calment was a fraud, or the acceleration of mortality force slowed down for advanced ages up to at least 120 years. Robine and Allard preferred to accept her authenticity, making them believe in a low rate of mortality at extreme age, and with it the prospect of human longevity increasing well into the future.

As Robine himself states it,

"By itself, the existence of Jeanne Calment provided as many arguments to question our knowledge of human longevity as the accumulation of thousands of centenarians." [19]

In 2018, Nikolay Zak followed up on a research suggestion from the gerontologist Valery Novoselov to review the longevity validation of Jeanne Calment. Novoselov, as an expert in geriatric phenotypes, had come to suspect that her claimed age of 122 at death was too good to be true [20, 21]. Motivated by Novoselov's thinking, Zak investigated the evidence for her validation as published by Michel Allard and Jean-Marie Robine around the time of her death in 1997 [4].

By the end of October 2018, Zak was convinced that the geriatrician's hunch was right. He had gathered enough information to deliver a talk and publish a paper refuting the longevity claim and supporting the alternative hypothesis that Jeanne Calment's daughter had taken her mother's identity on her death in 1934. She had then lived to 99 years old while claiming to be some 23 years older. Zak proposed inheritance and hypothetical insurance fraud as potential motives for the switch [22, 23, 24, 25].

The Calment affair that followed became a public controversy in France and abroad, with mixed but often hostile reactions from journalists [26, 27, 28, 29, 30, 31, 32, 33, 34].

During 2019 papers and statements were released by the original validators and their colleagues. They attempted to provide new evidence in favour of the validation and also to discredit Zak and his methods [36, 37, 38, 39, 40].

The organisation INSERM that had coordinated Calment's validation jointly with IPSEN foundation declared that the burden of proof lies with those who doubt the well established knowledge [35].

A Facebook counter-investigation group setup by residents of Arles where Mme Calment had lived sought to dig deeper into the case to prove that her longevity claim was authentic. The group published a list of points which they supposed to contradict the switch hypothesis [41].

It is our view that the response from Mme Calment's validators and other supporters did not successfully refute the evidence, yet the news media readily accepted it and declared the matter closed [42, 43, 44, 45, 46, 47].

Over the next four years, a small group of enthusiasts continued to investigate Calment's life in order to reconstruct in detail the picture of what happened. Here we present the outcome of that research, extending the previously published evidence [24, 48] and explaining how and why the mother and daughter might have exchanged places.

As we dive into Madame Calment's biography, we will look at each testimony in detail and discuss the arguments of the defenders of the record, so that any reader can form their own educated opinion. In our view the conclusion has moved overwhelmingly in favour of an identity switch, but there is no single point of evidence that provides the smoking gun.

We recognise that an informed consensus is therefore

difficult to reach within the community of demographers and gerontologists who have based so much of their research on the assumption of her validity. We continue to advocate for a DNA test to settle the matter conclusively.

In 2019 French authorities opened a case to determine if Yvonne and Jeanne's death certificates should be checked. After Zak highlighted the possibility of an identity switch, the Parquet de Tarascon commissioned Loïc Lalys, an anthropologist and French politician to write a report. Zak and his co-authors were not consulted for this study. Only Zak's preprint for his first paper was examined, while additional evidence available at the time was ignored.

According to press reports, Lalys dismissed Zak's analysis by saying that its references were unscientific [49, 50]. Our requests under the freedom of information act to see this hidden report have been ignored. The only public source of information is newspaper articles. Even the text of the press release issued to journalists is not available to us.

This cover-up needs to be seen against a backdrop in which life expectancy has not increased since 2010 as fast as many demographers had predicted. Annuity providers have made financial gains as a result, and they did so at the expense of pensioners [51].

Mme Calment became famous for her *viager* deal with a lawyer who continued to pay her the rent until his death. Customers' decision to buy an annuity depends on the estimate of their life expectancy. Naturally, insurance companies are keen to support researchers who are shifting this estimate by predicting a future increase in longevity, the longer the better. Coincidentally, such researchers are eager to provide Calment's age as a confirming example in their talks [8].

We believe that the French authorities should take the matter much more seriously, and that they must ensure that the DNA test needed to confirm or refute her authenticity is undertaken, even if it requires exhumation of Mme Calment and her close family's remains for the test.

The reason that Jeanne Calment's authenticity has been defended so vigorously by demographers is that so much depends on it. One of the scholars who initially insisted on the exhumation was Michel Poulain, an expert in longevity validation. He admitted that

> *"If tomorrow it is confirmed that it is a fake, a whole section of science would be called into question."* [52]

Robert Young, a consultant of the Guinness World Records (GWR) and director at the Gerontology Research Group (GRG) which maintains a much-cited database of the world's oldest people, told the Washington Post that

> *"Jeanne Calment is considered a golden standard of age validation, so challenging her is essentially challenging the validation standards. If you can show the number one person on the list is false - you kind of topple the whole system. And then you can interject yourself into the deal. No amount of paper validation would be sufficient."* [29]

The implications of Calment's longevity claim are much too important to be dismissed lightly. In our opinion a full and open public enquiry is called for.

We understand that Mme Calment's relatives, validators and supporters may be unhappy with Zak's hypothesis that she was not the record-breaking age she claimed. For our part, we do not judge her by her actions. We believe that she acted in the best interests of her family, and we leave it to others to consider whether she might have profited from age related benefits.

Nevertheless, the consequences of her longevity for science and society have been significant, and her actions have been inadvertently harmful if she is indeed inauthentic.

Zak has often been criticised for making accusations from a distance having never visited Arles or met Mme Calment. It is easier to see that the Earth is not flat from far away, and it is easier to see the problems in a longevity claim when not personally involved with the subject or the region. It is important to consider that the times and places in which Jeanne Calment lived were very different in many ways from how they are today, but this does not render us powerless to establish the truth.

Many local people have helped with our investigation, intentionally or otherwise. It is possible to find or order most relevant records online and we have enjoyed discovering a great deal about the people and history of Provence.

We observe that the Museon Arlaten in Arles no longer displays items related to the Calment family such as the bicycle which she abandoned in early 1960s after a fall due to the front wheel being braked too hard [53]. She was a vibrant part of the history of Arles and her story is of interest to visitors. We believe that her life and the Calment family should continue to be celebrated by the town.

It is important that the truth is reinstated. That is our only motive for this work. We wish to make it absolutely clear that we act in good faith. We urge readers to ignore any politics, personal attacks or appeals to authority from our opposition [19, 29, 37]. Only the evidence of events in the life of Jeanne Calment is important. That is what we focus on here.

Her fascinating life was covered by multiple layers of misinterpretations and misunderstandings but luckily it was possible to unravel the true story which in this case appears to be much more gripping than any fantasies.

This is an epic tale of how easily so many people can believe such an obvious falsehood, and it is a deep rabbit hole.

In the first volume we outline the biography of Mme Calment, describe the identity switch scenario, investigate the evolution of her signatures, and figure out who had tuberculosis.

The second volume is devoted to untangling Jeanne's and Yvonne's lives through the examination and analysis of Mme Calment's testimony, lifestyle, photographic and other evidence.

Those who think they have a counterargument which refutes the switch, have good chances of finding it in the third volume, where we review the counterclaims from the various proponents of Mme Calment's longevity. We conclude with a weighted table of evidence and a chronology of the "Calment affair".

A Postscript, devoted to Jesus Christ, Van Gogh, and the Jewish princes will highlight parallels between the Calment case and stories from the past.

We are also going to publish our research into the biographies of other validated supercentenarians in a separate book.

We present a lot of images for Jeanne Calment and her family. For some of them, found in newspapers, on postcards, or websites the original source is unknown. Sometimes a comparison with photographs of undisputed provenance allows us to be certain of their authenticity. We acknowledge cases where they can't be verified with absolute confidence.

We also give a lot of newspaper extracts and genealogic information (which is often available online at the department archives of Bouches-du-Rhône https://www.archives13.fr/) without always citing sources inline so as not to overload the text.

METHOD

You can talk with any scholar, who would say, we would not accept this even from a student! It's not scientific, there's no methodology, no hypothesis, no nothing. It's just, like, a document, bringing more sentences to say Jeanne Calment is not Jeanne Calment.

J.-M. Robine [29]

T he essence of the Calment affair is the competition of two alternatives histories, two scenarios (switch and no switch) of the past. The Bayesian method we use to unravel the true history was outlined in [48].

We have tried our best to collect all the relevant information and then used it to describe the scenarios and to estimate their relative likelihood. To do this, we have broken down the evidence into 57 facts, each of which is evaluated as a hypothesis within a scenario in question.

Some of the evidence is not reliable enough to be used for analysis. For example, the claim that Mme Calment's father (and not her husband) was involved in the *anti-*

German league during the WWI could be viewed as pro-switch, but we know this from journalist Jean-Claude Lamy citing local historian René Garagnon, and not from the audio recording of Mme Calment herself.

Other evidence, like her revelations about Hitler, is irrelevant to the switch. Nevertheless, we try to present as much information as possible, so that the reader can enjoy the whole picture of this amazing story.

Our prior perceptions are reflected in the first hypothesis of the [1]*Long life* in the *no switch* scenario vs not so long life in the *switch* scenario. Here the likelihood ratio of 10 million in favour of the switch is an objective measure of the higher a priori probability to live to the age of 99 rather than 122 [38, 48].

The relative likelihood for the following facts is evaluated in sequential order, taking into account all preceding information. Some hypotheses can be considered independent from previous knowledge, while others can't.

For example, our assessment of the plausibility of Calment's [2]*Signatures* in either scenario is not affected by the duration of her life while when analyzing the credibility of her [3]*Identity card* we consider the set of known samples of Jeanne's signatures as part of the scenario under study.

Similarly, when assessing the plausibility of the hypothesis that Yvonne [57]*Avoided being caught,* we consider her [55]*Decision to masquerade in 1932* as part of the *switch* scenario.

17

In the *no switch* scenario, the hypothesis that Jeanne was strikingly healthy at an old age is heavily correlated to her unique longevity. Thus, we assess the relative probability for her [39]*Exceptional health* given the prior [1]*Long life* as just 1.5 in favour of the switch.

When evaluating [37]*Slipping into being Yvonne,* we list some of the already considered slips but only take into account those not previously mentioned.

The Bayesian analysis in the end of volume 2 can be used as a weighted list of evidence. The likelihood ratios there reflect our view of the relative strength of the considered facts. Some of the evidence ([38]*Selectivity of memories,* [55]*Decision to masquerade in 1932,* [56]*Decision to masquerade after Jeanne's death,* [57]*Avoiding being caught*) is complex and incorporates information discussed in several chapters, including those devoted to the counterclaims from our opponents.

The considered probabilistic measure is naturally subjective, so the reader is invited to form his own judgement. We believe that the gap is so wide that any differences are highly unlikely to influence the overall conclusion.

Strict adherence to the method should help to avoid pitfalls, such as counting same evidence multiple times. It is important to disregard the perception of the plausibility of a given scenario while evaluating the relative likelihood of each fact: the considered scenario should be assumed to be true, no matter how unlikely it seems.

In the absence of the correct methodology, a researcher can suffer from various psychological biases. For example, the order in which information is assessed can have an impact on judgement. After being exposed to compelling evidence in favour of one of the competing scenarios, our brain dismisses the alternative scenario. Because of this prior knowledge, we subconsciously ignore information that contradicts our belief. Such biases have been known to result in experts giving wrong assessments in court [54].

Our estimate of the overall likelihood ratio for the available *anti-switch* evidence is 8 billion to one in favour of *no switch*. When facing such strong evidence, one should not forget the so-called *Cromwell rule* which warns us not to assign a prior probability to zero or one – we should never be absolutely certain if we are dealing with real life and not a mathematical statement [55].

In history, unlike mathematics, the proofs are probabilistic, so it is important not to jump to premature conclusions. Despite the solid weight of proofs against substitution, the arguments in its favour turned out to be more than a trillion times stronger.

Bayes' rule was invoked in 1899 by the eminent mathematician Henri Poincaré when he acted as an expert in the famous *Dreyfus Affair* and denounced a *"colossal error"* in the prosecution's methodology. Bayesian inference was also used by French artillery in the WWI when Henri's cousin Raymond was president of the French Republic, and later by Alan Turing working on the Enigma project during WWII to estimate the probability of a hypothesis when information arrives piecemeal [56] [57].

The Bayesian method is now widespread in forensic science, and there are guidelines for its competent use in court [58]. Such a rigorous analysis was important in the early stages of the *Calment Affair* when the information available was much scarcer than today. It is the lack of correct methodology which led the initial validators and their followers to consider each document mentioning Jeanne Calment as an independent piece of evidence and to ignore numerous confusions in her testimony.

We consider that analyses such as ours can be applied to various other historical controversies in the future.

Jeanne Calment

ORIGINS

Extraordinary longevity of Jeanne Calment is due to an exceptional genetic inheritance, randomly accumulated within the social group of craftsmen and shopkeepers running prosperous businesses in the town.

J.-M. Robine and Michel Allard [4]

Arles is one of the oldest French cities, it got the name Arelate (meaning "on the marsh" in Celtic) several centuries BCE. The name proved to catch the essence. A 1756 travel guide noted that Arles is almost surrounded by a morass making its air unhealthy [59]. In 1817 French historian Amédée Pichot (1795-1877) had published a thesis *"The diseases caused by the marshes of Arles"*.

In 1889 Vincent Van Gogh wrote to his brother Theo from there:

"Here the so-called good town of Arles is a funny place which for good reasons friend Gauguin calls the filthiest place in the south." [60]

Arlesians were suffering from various epidemics, from

22

Black Death to cholera and tuberculosis throughout the history of their town, and the theme of the disease is a key element of our story.

On the other hand, it was argued that

> *"There is no city in France so remarkable for antiquities as Arles, insomuch that it is generally called a second Rome."* [59]

According to the famous Arlesian historian and mayor Émile Fassin (1842-1922),

> *"A fallen city, such as Arles, which takes title from its past and draws all its grandeur from its memories should never lightly touch the monuments that hold this grandeur."*

The daughter-in-law of Fassin's sister-in-law, the oldest human, Doyenne of humanity, Jeanne Louise Calment (1875-1997), a *"purebred Arlesian"* as she called herself [61] is one of such monuments.

Jeanne Calment was born on 21 February 1875 at 5 rue du Roure in the Roquette sector of Arles. In the Middle Ages this district of fishermen and craftsmen was called the *"Bourg des Porcelets"* after the noble family who oversaw it from their castle. The castle was later swallowed by the city, but arguably left a circular anomaly which can still be traced on the modern plan of Arles [62].

It is often said that Jeanne was born into a bourgeois family with servants to take care of the household chores, but this is not quite true. Her father was the last in a line of marine carpenters who built boats to transport goods on the river Rhône. For over a century her Calment ancestors had lived in La Roquette and by the quays in Trinquetaille on the other side of the river working hard to earn their living.

They married into the families of other tradesmen including bakers, millers, sailors, wheel-rights, and shoemakers. They were skilled craftsmen but were not highly educated and their lifestyle did not include live-in servants, the hallmark of the bourgeoisie.

The poet Frédéric Mistral believed that the Calment name came from the word *"calaman"* meaning a wooden beam in the Provençal dialect that he cherished [63]. He knew they had been carpenters, but we can trace the Calment paternal line back to long before the time when they mastered their trade as builders of wooden ships.

In the 15th century Garin Calmenc owned land and vineyards near Pouzilhac 50km North of Arles. He is the earliest known direct ancestor in the Calment family's patronymic line according to records available on Geneanet.

The small town of Pouzilhac was dominated by a castle that had been gifted to the runners up for the French throne, the powerful Dukes of Uzès, by King Philip IV in the late XIII century. How the family Calmenc came there is uncertain, but Kalman is a Yiddish derivative of the name Kalonymos which had been used by a family of Jewish Nesi'im (princes) in Occitania for centuries.

The town of Uzès hosted a small community of Jewish scholars who likely included some of the remnants of the

Kalonymos family. In 1297 the Jews of Uzès were accused of a ritual infanticide [64] and a decade later all the Jews were expelled from France whose border passed nearby at that time.

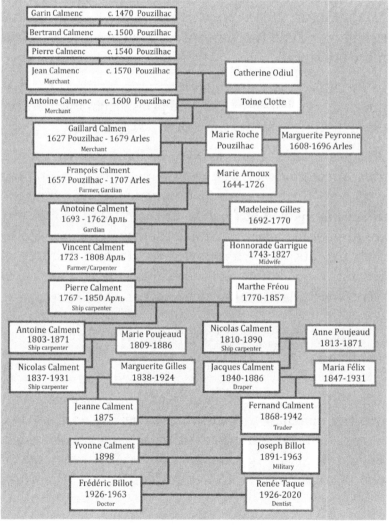

The Calments

Jeanne's ancestors could have been forced to convert and take refuge in Pouzilhac 15km to the east. Regardless of where they came from, the castle vicinity provided the first converted Calmenques a convenient place to shake off their past. This version of the name Kalman with a twang in the end was probably chosen because it sounds more Provençal.

In Pouzilhac the Calmenque/Calmenc family thrived as masons, merchants, tailors, and priests, looking after the Catholic Church by the walls of the castle.

300 years later around 1675 Gaillard Calmen (great-great-great grandson of Garin Calmenc) built strong ties with Arles through trade and his godchildren: by the end of his life, he had at least 16 of them there. Some were children of his relatives while others were abandoned by their parents. Gaillard followed the ancient tradition of philanthropy coming from the times when his ancestors were Jewish. As Fernand once told Madame Calment,

> "You give, you give, and you have no recognition." [65]

The XVII century Pouzilhac was not a safe place for wealthy merchants. Once while travelling with his two mules, Gaillard was attacked by a gang of horsemen. They stole his animals but gave one back in exchange for two pistoles (around 20 livres according to "The Three Musketeers") [66].

That was too much for Gaillard, so he decided to relocate and join the stable community of his Calmen relatives who prospered as merchants and tailors in Arles. He requested consent from the town council to settle [67], and so his Calment descendants would live in the ancient town for over three centuries surviving the droughts, floods, epidemics, and other challenges that troubled their lives.

After the first wife of Gaillard died, he remarried a tailor's widow Marguerite Peyronne and settled at her ranch in the Camargue surrounded by flamingo lagoons and mosquito swamps. Marguerite was 19 years older than Gaillrd, but he died 17 years earlier at the age of 52.

Gaillard brought with him three children born in Pouzilhac: Jean, François, and Antoine. Antoine became a priest and so was childless. Jean became a master tailor, the profession common among his relatives who already lived in Arles, but none of his children survived.

François Calmenc and his sons became land workers, taking care of bulls and horses. They were called *Gardians* and lived around the St. Laurent parish near the place where Jeanne Calment would be born five generations later.

Jeanne's grandson Freddy Billot in the Gardian costume, 1930

Founded in 1512, the *Brotherhood of the Gardians* is the oldest of this kind still present in France today. It was responsible for helping the elderly, poor and disabled.

The Gardians lived and dressed like cowboys, riding the horses in the windy saline plains of Western Europe's largest river delta while rounding the *taureaux* for the corrida held at the Roman arena in Arles.

In 1720 the *Great Plague of Marseille* killed every fourth person in the region but thanks to their mobility the Gardians were able to seek refuge outside of the town. Antoine Calmen and his wife Madeleine Gilles survived and in 1723 their son Vincent was born.

When Vincent married Honnorade Garrigue in 1763, he was almost 40 years old, but the wedding act stated he was only 34 – an uncommon occurrence in France where a marriage record is not in line with the birth and death act (Vincent died age 85 in 1808).

Honorade was a daughter of a very wealthy farmer Jean Garrigue from the Mas Neuf aux Sansouires and a midwife Elisabeth Aubert. The pair settled at the Mas Neuf and their nine children were born there but most of them died in infancy.

Like his great-grandfather Gaillard, Vincent also had multiple godchildren, most of whom were brought into life by his wife who had a long and distinguished career as a midwife in Arles. Honnorade helped her daughter-in-law Marthe Freou give birth to Jeanne's grandfather Antoine on Prairial 30 of the XI year of the French Republic (June 19th, 1803). It was her granddaughter Honorade Calment, also a midwife, who helped Jeanne's mother Marguerite Gilles to be born in 1838.

Vincent was the first in the family who mastered the profession of carpenter. He taught his son Pierre how to make *sabots*, the Gardians' wooden clogs. These shoes resembled miniature barges known as *chalands* and *penelles* navigating the Rhône. The boats would descend the river with their cargos from mines and quarries, using the flow of the current with large paddles at the rear to guide them. Once emptied at their destination they had to be hauled back up by teams of horses provided by the Gardians on the riverbanks.

Pierre went further and became the founder of the Calment shipbuilder dynasty. He married Marthe Freou, daughter of a shoemaker, and the couple settled in La Roquette just a hundred meters away from the house where their great-granddaughter Jeanne would live with her parents three generations later.

Pierre had nine children including four sons Vincent, Antoine, Jacques, and Nicolas who followed his steps in the boat construction business. Antoine and Nicolas married sisters Marie Anne and Anne. Both were daughters of a baker Jean François Poujaud who owned an oven at rue du Four Banal on the other side of the Rhône.

The brothers settled there at the Trinquetaille quay, and their shipbuilding business continued to prosper.

Jeanne's father Nicolas was born to Antoine and Marie Anne in 1837. He married a neighbour, Marguerite Gilles, and she gave birth to their first son Antoine in 1862. Next year they had a daughter Marie who lived only three days. In 1865 their second boy François was born and two years later Antoine died at the age of five.

Marguerite Gilles, unconfirmed   Marguerite Gilles and Nicolas Calment

In 1875 the family moved to the Roquette district where grandfather Pierre had started his shipbuilding career. Nicolas was one of the last and most successful in the Calment dynasty of carpenters. In 1880 he was chosen as a partner of the *Alais au Rhône* railway and navigation company, which planned to use a fleet of barges to transport coal to the sea.

Nicolas had built multiple chalands but in 1885 had to resell them to other customers because the company that had commissioned them went bankrupt.

Sailing ships at the port of Arles in 1880

They had ambitious plans for expansion but in 1885 Nicolas' partner Jean Baptiste Calment died and as time passed those same railways that brought him business were becoming a commercial threat to the river traffic. Nicolas seems to have taken the opportunity to quit while he was ahead.

He built his last ship when Jeanne was a young girl in the 1880s and invested the money in property. The family bought a large house at 53 rue de la Roquette, and a farm, the *Mas de Rourion* in the sparsely populated community of Saint-Martin-de-Crau ten miles East of Arles. Later Nicolas enjoyed making wine there.

After settling into their new home, the Calments employed Marguerite Minaud, a cousin of Jeanne's mother, as a live-in domestic. One of her main duties would be to walk the young Jeanne to school and back.

Jeanne began her education at a time of new opportunity, but also of disruption. Secular schools provided by the municipal council sprang up to meet the new requirements for obligatory primary education, but the religious schools also continued to operate until 1903.

Jeanne's parents were devoted Catholics, so they chose one of the best fee-paying schools, run by Mme Benet-Coste at rue de la Calade. The headmistress was soon accused in participation of her students in the royalists' gatherings and suspended from her position, but she was able to return several years later. In 1884 the studies were disrupted further by the last cholera outbreak in the town.

After passing her First Communion in the Coste school, Jeanne entered the secondary courses for girls which had recently opened on rue St. Paul. This school soon moved to rue du Cloître next to the church of Saint Trophimus.

Jeanne was something of a tomboy in her youth, the opposite of her brother François. Their father would say *"Ma fille est le garçon, et mon garçon est la fille"* –

"My girl is the boy, and my boy is the girl,"

but XIX century France was a man's world with few opportunities for women. François joined the navy and went on faraway expeditions, while Jeanne's energies were channelled into art and music. She was gifted in both and continued to paint and play piano after leaving school at 16.

Interestingly, Jeanne's future husband also came from the Calment family. Nicolas had a double cousin Jacques

Calment who was three years younger. Their fathers Antoine and Nicolas were brothers, and their mothers were sisters, making them first cousins on both sides of their families.

Shipbuilder Nicolas Calment   His son Jacques, trader

Children of the elder brother, Antoine, became mariners and carpenters while Jacques and his brothers Pierre, Claude and Adolphe Claudius benefitted from education which became more widespread in their time. They seemed set to follow their father into the ship building trade, but ended up choosing to become traders, accountants, and insurance agents.

Jacques started as a draper's assistant, selling cloth at a time when many people would still sew their own clothes. Among the shop's customers was Maria Félix, one of four sisters who were heirs to a property fortune.

Maria Felix (?) and Yvonne Calment, 1904

Maria's sister Antoinette married Emile Fassin, a successful lawyer and much-admired local historian who was elected mayor of Arles in 1878. Jacques was not such a powerful catch, but Maria was passionate about fashion and saw him as the perfect partner to help launch her own ambitious plans.

As the end of the empire was approaching, her father Mathieu Félix (despite having daughters named Maria and Antoinette) and her brothers-in-law Jambon and Fassin became republicans. They were happy with her engagement which suited the new ideology of liberty, equality, and fraternity.

The couple married in 1868 and had a son Fernand Calment the same year. With financial support from her father, Maria helped Jacques open his own shop overlooking the triangular place des Porcelets on rue Royale, soon to be renamed rue de la République.

There is a legend that the Porcelet family started with astonishing fertility when a mother had 9 boys born on the same day, just like a pig – hence the family name and the piglets carved in the stone of their castle.

In the fifteenth century French *Parlement* considered the towers in recently annexed Provence as potentially aggressive, so it ordered their truncation to the level of the surrounding roof. The relatively small Porcelet tower apparently survived and is now visible on aerial images of the former Maison Calment.

In Gaillard Calment's time, the tower was painted by the Arlesian architect Jacques Peytret just to the right of the flood-proof boat bridge that had connected Arles with its suburb Trinquetaille across the Rhône since antiquity. In 1882 a similar boat bridge in Saint-Gilles was repaired by Jean-Baptiste Calment, a cousin and partner of Jeanne's father.

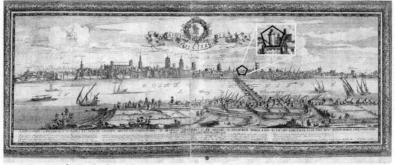

Porcelet-Calment tower in 1660 by Jacques Peytret

In 1881, using Maria's dowry, Jacques Calment bought the house belonging to her paternal grandmother Anne Roux at 3, rue de la Poissonnerie, and extended his store. The fast-growing business required bookkeeping, and this was done by Jacques' brother Claudius.

GRANDS MAGASINS DE NOUVEAUTÉS

Jacques CALMENT

de la Poissonnerie, Rue Gambetta et rue de la République

ARLES

BOUCHES-DU-RHONE

A. Floren et Cie 6, Boul. des Italiens, Paris Londres

A postcard from Maison Calment, 1880s

Place des Porcelets was a good location, but the streets were narrow and overshadowed by old buildings.

In the 1870s the municipal government of Arles saw a need to improve traffic through the town. The boat bridge to Trinquetaille over the Rhône was replaced by a metal one in the year when Jeanne was born. To improve access, the town council decided to run a wide road straight by the point where Jacques had his shop. They authorised compulsory purchase of property that stood in the way of the new street, including the Calment's.

In 1883 the route pierced the town, emerging onto place des Porcelets which was then cleared of old buildings so that the new rue Gambetta opened into a larger space at the bend to the Trinquetaille bridge.

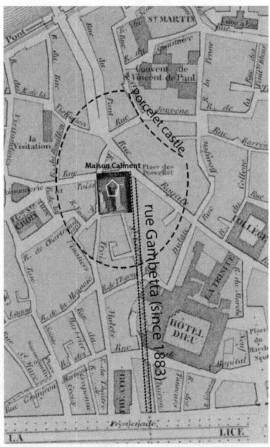

1871 map by Auguste Véran

The Calment shop benefitted well from the new plan. With impressively rebuilt facades onto the corner of the new road, rue Gambetta, it was a prime location for commerce. In 1884 the council put it up for auction by the traditional method of accepting the highest bid submitted before a candle burns out. Calment competed with Jean Baptiste Gilles and the price went up from 10000 to 19100 francs during the trade.

The Calment shop around 1900

Jacques won the auction, giving him back his much-improved shop and two floors of apartments above. The spacious property featured the ancient round tower that was once a guard post for the Porcelet castle.

In preparation for the centenary celebration of the French Revolution, the enlarged square was renamed from place des Porcelets to place d'Antonelle after the

Jacobin first mayor of Arles.

Marquis d'Antonelle was also President of the jurors of the Revolutionary Court that ruled against Queen Marie Antoinette of Austria and an architect of the attachment of the former Papal state *Comtat Venaissin* to France, but a descendant of the Porcelets, Emile Fassin was not quite content with such a decision:

> *"A fallen city, such as ours, which takes title from its past and draws all its grandeur from its memories, should never lightly touch the monuments that hold this grandeur; these are precious titles, which deserve as much care as those which we keep with such jealous vigilance in the municipal archives. Scratching an historic name on the frontispiece of a street, without necessity, or disfiguring a medieval building by completely modern arrangements are also regrettable acts.*
>
> *Now, there was, it seems, no reason to dethrone the Porcelets, one of the purest glories of our city. Relegating them, as we did, to rue de la Poissonnerie, is – forgive me the word – a kind of impropriety. Their name was to remain attached to their former stronghold, on the site of the feudal manor so renowned in our annals.*
>
> *As for Marquis d'Antonelle, does he not seem to be well landscaped in this district where nothing recalls his memory? Was not his place, on the contrary, quite indicated at the Revolutionary quarter, rue de la Roquette where his house still*

remains?

However, place des Porcelets, considerably enlarged by the demolition of the island 97 and by the annexation of a section of rue du Théâtre, constituted a new creation, which required a new name; we wanted this name to carry with it the commemoration of the Centenary and thus to fix the date of an embellishment of our city.

Therefore, the place des Porcelets is now called Place d'Antonelle. Besides, the expropriated ones were compensated: the neighbouring street, rue de la Poissonnerie, took the name of Porcelets – 'Non erat hic locus', we could say in a nutshell. If there remains any respect for the historical tradition, it would be at rue Saint-Estève that their names are given." [68]

By tragic coincidence, just after the historic refurbishment of his shop, Jacques fell victim to a typhoid outbreak in 1886, leaving the business to his widow Maria and young son Fernand, who was finishing his studies in the Arles college. An obituary in the local newspaper said:

"Last Thursday, death took away, in the prime of life, one of our most generally esteemed compatriots. Mr. Jacques Calment, merchant and former judge at the commercial court, succumbed to the effects of a cruel illness.

Son of his deeds, Mr. Jacques Calment had acquired by his work and his intelligence a distinguished place among his brothers, and death has caught him at the head of an important enterprise, to which he had given a truly extraordinary extension for our city."

Another obituary gives an account of the funeral:

"A large crowd escorted the coffin to its final resting place, testifying by its sad appearance to the respect and universal sympathy earned by the deceased. As the funeral procession made its way along, we saw tears welling up in many people's eyes. We firmly believe that the unanimous sorrow of the people of Arles can somewhat ease the immense pain of the Calment family, so cruelly affected by this circumstance. Two of our city's musical ensembles, the Philharmonia and the Arlésienne, of which the deceased was an honoured member, led the procession, playing the darkest melodies from their repertoire.

Three funeral palls preceded the coffin, which disappeared under the many wreaths offered by relatives and friends. The first was carried by the main cloth merchants of our city, the second by the employees of the deceased and the other by the delegates of the 'Cercle de l'Avenir'. The bearers of the most beautiful and large wreaths stood before each pall, two of which were offered by the staff of the house and the rest by the Arlésienne Musical Society, M. Tassy, and the Cercle de l'Avenir.

Mourning was led by the son and brother of the deceased. At the grave Monsieur Nicquet gave a speech which made a profound impression on those present:

'I have come to do an incredibly sad duty, bringing with a few parting words an expression of our shared sorrow and deep regret at learning that we have just lost someone whose love was so dear to us. The last day you were with us was a wonderful day of Easter. 'I leave you for a while,' you said, but death, that invincible, jealous reaper, has already chosen its victim; so today we are in the presence of your mortal remains, hidden from us by that cold and indifferent coffin.

Death, my dear friend, came to you when a future full of laughter opened before you, when you gathered everything that makes a man happy: wealth, health, and fortune. Indeed, from your youth we saw how you started out as a simple employee; later you took charge of the drapery store you founded; finally, by joining forces with the most respected family, we saw how you, through the intelligence, hard work, delicacy, and frankness of your procedures, created one of the first houses in our town.

The Arlesian trade community appreciated your qualities so much that it was not long before you became a judge of its Court. In conducting these functions, very honorable but also exceedingly difficult and delicate, you have shown common sense and a firm will, using only impartial and stern justice, leaving aside any favoritism.

And just when you, by your work, had erected a pedestal on which you were to find the reward of your labors, securing a peaceful old age in the future, the mysterious fate that always tries to make one feel how small he is in this world, came to take you prematurely from the affections of your family and your friends.

Despite your separation from us, the memory of you will never fade from our hearts, and the large crowd that accompanied you to your final resting place proves how much you have won everyone's friendship and sympathy. May this token of respect be a relief to your widow and your son from their pain. Jacques Calment, our friend, farewell for the last time, farewell.'"

Jacques left an estate worth over a million Euros at today's value, and the store continued to prosper.

French society was male dominated, so the shop was expected to have a man in charge, but it was Maria who had to be the driving force of the business while Fernand learnt the trade.

One of the largest wreaths at the funeral was offered by M. Tassy who was Jacques' neighbour and business partner. Their shops worked closely together and made joint announcements, for example that they were going to close their doors at midday, Sundays, and holidays from January 1st, 1886. After Jacques' death the press sometimes referred to their stores as a united *"Maison Calment-Tassy"*.

However, Tassy went bankrupt in 1899, divorced with his wife in 1903, and left Arles. Maison Calment, led by Maria and Fernand with the help of Jacques' brother Claudius, would stay afloat much longer.

Meanwhile Jeanne Calment had blossomed into a beautiful young Arlésienne. A letter from Maria Félix to her sister Anne Antoinette (wife of Emile Fassin), preserved in Arles Médiathèque, indicates that Maria was not certain that Jeanne was a suitable match but approved the choice of her son.

Sisters Antoinette and Maria (unconfirmed)

"Arles, 15th June 1895

Dear Antoinette,

Fassin must have passed on the letter that Fernand wrote to him announcing his desire to marry Jeanne Calment the daughter of Nicolas Calment the cousin. I wanted to let a few more days pass before writing you to make sure that it was really serious.

He had said that his ideas have been around for a long time and that his affection is shared. I think I can only comply with his wishes. As I was finishing my letter Fernand told me about the one that he had just received from you. You cannot believe the pleasure it has given us, knowing that his choice is approved by all of us. He asks me to thank his dear uncle for all his kind words.

The proposal will be made this evening for the wedding. It will not be before next spring. Fernand and I are happy to have good news of Paul and we hope that he will be back soon. Farewell dear Antoinette, I kiss you with all my heart.

Your sister, Maria Calment"

In 1896 Fernand and Jeanne married with a special dispensation from the church because they were double second cousins. Nicolas' success had already levitated his family to the petty (petit) bourgeois, the self-made middle class with pretentions of status. At 21 years old, his daughter Jeanne had finally become by marriage part of the *haute bourgeoisie* with inherited status. Through charity, she rubbed shoulders with what was left of the nobility and would never have any need to work.

Jeanne Calment

THE IDENTITY
SWITCH

To substantiate the claim of substitution, a solid screenplay should be put up, a genuine thriller, and this is not easy, if not impossible.

M. Allard and J.-M. Robine [1]

Fernand, Jeanne and Yvonne. Crouanson's collection

wo years after the marriage of Jeanne and Fernand Calment, the couple's only daughter Yvonne was born on 19th January 1898, and the scene was set for an extraordinary series of events. Exactly 36 years later the household announced her funeral, but was it really Yvonne who was laid to rest, or had in fact the mother Jeanne died instead?

We know for sure that one of two things happened. Either Yvonne died from tuberculosis and Jeanne Calment lived on to become the world's oldest ever verified person by a significant margin of three years, or Yvonne switched identities with her mother, faked her own death in place of Jeanne's and went on to fool the whole world for 63 more years. Both are extraordinary stories. One of them is true.

Here we will trace the details of the switch as we suppose it could have unfolded. It will become clear how we think the motivation developed. This will be followed by the evidence that leads us to believe that this is the correct history.

When Dr. Lébre asked Madame Calment if she was comfortable living in her husband's house, she slipped:

"Of course! My parents were well off!" [65] (25 May 1994 10:40).

While Fernand brought the best local teachers to help Jeanne developing her passions for art and music, Yvonne was grown up spoilt by servants who would follow her bidding. She was also instructed in painting and piano, but she did not have her mother's natural talent.

As her only son took responsibility for the drapery business, Maria indulged her granddaughter with her interest in clothes and fashion. Being a pretty girl, Yvonne enjoyed balls and celebrations which gave her the opportunity to show off her original dresses while Fernand was involved in organising these festivals.

Yvonne in St. Trophime, 1923

Yvonne also accompanied her father to horse races and bullfights, but over time she grew bored of the mundane life in the polite society of Arles. In her childhood, Maria and Fernand instilled in Yvonne a sense of adventure with outings in the country, which later became her major passion.

According to local press, both Maria and Jeanne had for many years supported groups that gave aid to wounded and sick soldiers, including the *Association des Dames Françaises of Arles* established in 1897 under the leadership of Mme Hadron, the future mother-in-law of Marshal Philippe Pétain.

Nicolas Calment was a councillor known at the time for his controversial job of distributing benefits for the poor in the *"Bureau du Bienfaisance"* located in the Arles hospital Hôtel-Dieu. Jeanne followed in the steps of her father. In 1907 she was listed as advisor at a society of mutual help for workers in Arles led by Countess Divonne.

Successful bourgeois, the Calments willingly participated in charity activities that were not limited to local initiatives: in 1905 they sent donations through the Red Cross to the French Embassy in St. Petersburg for the widows of Russian soldiers killed in the Russo-Japanese War.

During the First World War Yvonne's school at rue du Cloître was used as a hospital supervised by *l'Union des Femmes de France* while the girls studied in the premises of a nearby maternal school. The Calments participated in various Red Cross projects such as *"Linge du Soldat"* at the hospital and *"Cantine du Soldat"* at the Arles station.

Union des Femmes de France, Arles station, WWI

During the war, soldiers were suffering not only from their wounds but also from diseases such as tuberculosis. It was a deadly threat also for those who took care of them. Doctor Louis Rey created a tuberculosis dispensary at the hospital and the Calment family doctor, Jules Urpar, fell victim to the disease in 1915.

This could be how Yvonne caught the infection, a decade before her marriage in 1926. Tuberculosis was stigmatised as a disease of the poor working class. Jeanne was in denial. She blamed Yvonne's sickness on Maria and the common myth that a chest infection can be caught from cold shock and dampness. In 1993 Madame Calment (MC) recited the story as if she had learned it by heart a long time ago.

Audio recordings [65] (25 and 26 Feb 1993 19:50)	Translation
MC: C´est à la suite d'une pleurésie; c'est ma belle-mère qui en est la cause; quand elle était petite, ma belle-mère, comme elle a eu qu'un garçon, une fille elle était heureuse. Elle l'avait tellement couverte, tellement couverte! Nous avions une campagne à Bord du Rhône. A l'époque on baignait dans les eaux du Rhône. Elle aimait beaucoup pour y aller. Il fallait aller à pied. Elle l'avait tellement couverte quand elle arriva, elle a transpiré. Elle l'a trempé dans l'eau toute transpirante, quand elle est sortie elle a grelotté; c'est partie de là, c'est ma belle-mère qui en est la cause.	MC: It was the result of pleurisy; my mother-in-law is the cause. When she was little, my mother-in-law, as she only had a boy, she was happy with a girl. She kept her covered so much, so much in her cover! We had a country house on the Rhône. We bathed in the waters of the Rhône. She loved to go there. You had to go on foot. She kept her covered so much that when she arrived, she sweated. She dipped her in the water all sweaty, when she came out, she shivered; it went from there, my mother-in-law is the cause.

The interviewer asked if that happened where Jeanne's father built his boats and Madame Calment agreed. In fact, the ships were made in the Barriol quarter, which was not suitable for children's vacations.

In 1907 the Félix sisters including Maria inherited from their parents the *Mas de Prentegarde* to the south of Arles and most likely Yvonne was bathing there. The name *"Prends-te-garde"* means "beware" and refers to the dangerous flooding into the area and even the house itself from the Rhône.

Despite her disease, Yvonne got engaged with Captain Joseph Billot, but their marriage was delayed until she was 28 and Joseph was almost 35 years old: he was in the army while she was ill.

Yvonne was young and strong. The form of tuberculosis she had initially may have been extra-pulmonary, perhaps an infection of her eyes and nose which became latent after some basic treatment. During this time Joseph pursued a successful career in the army. In 1925 he got an honourable distinction, and his father Paul received a medal from Pope Pius XI:

"Arles. Double distinction. We address our sincere congratulations to our compatriot M. Joseph Billot, captain of the 63rd artillery, who has just been named Knight of the Legion of Honour with this beautiful citation:

'Since the end of the 1914-1918 war, he has never stopped campaigning, having served 2 years in the Rhineland, 14 months in the Levant and

25 months in Morocco. During this whole period, as well as during the war, he has always stood out for his qualities of dedication and courage, particularly in the battle of Aoudour, on May 2, 1925, where, in command of the isolated escort battery, he led the fight, ensuring the safety and continuity of the fire.'

By a happy coincidence, almost on the same day, the Sovereign Pontiff, on the request which had been transmitted to him by the archbishop, awarded to Mr. Paul Billot, father of the new knight, the Bene merenti medal for the exceptional and purely gracious services which he has not ceased to render, for the last 40 years, to his adopted parish.

Gifted with a magnificent voice that time has not been able to weaken, he has given, without ever tiring, to our religious ceremonies their most beautiful splendour, and it is our pleasure to offer him, on this occasion, with our affectionate compliments, the expression of our deepest gratitude."

Joseph was born on March 7th, 1891, in the old house at Place du Sauvage where the names of all the family members were engraved on the stone. His grandfather Frédéric Florentin Billot was a distinguished lawyer and a prolific writer who published numerous books and articles on diverse subjects including a new system of navigation across the seas.

He also petitioned the Senate against "living burials" in the hope of preventing the tragedies that occurred when people were inadvertently placed in a coffin and buried alive after misdiagnosing their death.

In 1861 he even received a personal letter from Pope Pius IX. This Pope became famous for declaring the infallibility of his office in a way of confronting criticism akin to Calment's validators' response to research questioning her identity.

In 1865, Frédéric Florentin Billot was a member of the Arles city council, together with shipbuilder Nicolas Calment (Jacques' father), wealthy landowner Mathieu Félix (Jacques' father-in-law), Augustin Tardieu and Amédée Gay (future mayors of Arles), draper Adolphe Lalmand, and other politicians of the time.

Lalmand was Calments' neighbour at rue Royale (future rue de la République) in 1876. His father Nathan was friends with Pierre Fassin, father of Jacques' future brother-in-law. Lalmands might have employed Calment in the beginning of his career before he met Maria and opened his own shop.

Fassin and Felix descended from the nobility, but they supported the revolution which was supposed to bring more equality. Billot, on the other hand, was a royalist. He didn't leave much money to his heirs and after his death in 1868 the family requested a scholarship for the college of his son Paul. They justified this request by the honours of Paul's maternal grandfather, Jean Julien Estrangin (1788-1848) who was also a famous lawyer, politician, and historian of Arles.

In 1926 *La Croix de Provence* congratulated Paul's wife Marie Jouve on being awarded a medal of national recognition for raising five children: Albert, Jean-Paul, Thérèse, Antoinette, and their elder brother, captain Joseph Billot, a knight of the Legion of Honour, who had recently married Mlle Yvonne Calment in Saint Trophime.

Arrondissement d'Arles

Arles. — *La médaille de la reconnaissance nationale* vient d'être décernée à Mme Billot, pour les cinq enfants qu'elle a élevés, et dont l'aîné M. le capitaine Billot, chevalier de la Légion d'honneur, épousait récemment, à Saint-Trophime, Mlle Yvonne Calment. Nos sincères félicitations.

Marie Jouve and Paul Billot   Their daughter Nenette

Paul Billot's selflessness and dedication to the religion
were noted in his obituary of 1930:

> *"District of Arles, St-Julien. Our parish has just
> suffered a very painful loss in the person of Mr.
> Paul Billot, who died on 23 July. Gifted with
> a magnificent voice, he sang, for more than 50
> years, at all our services, with a fidelity that never
> wavered and an absolute disinterestedness.*
>
> *The son of a renowned lawyer in our town and
> attached by his mother to the Estrangin family,
> which is one of the most noble in our country, he did
> not believe that he was falling from grace by taking
> his place at the lectern as a cantor would have done,*

and the happiness of his life, his greatest joy, was to devote himself in this way to God and religion.

A few years ago, Pope Pius XI awarded him the medal "Bene merenti", and this was for him the most precious of all awards. We bow to his memory, which will always be dear to us, and we express to his family, who mourn him, our feelings of deep sorrow and religious sympathy."

Billots and the Popes, 1861-1930

Jeanne was much younger than her in-laws. It was said that when Paul Billot paid her a visit on the occasion of Joseph's engagement, he had taken the mother for the daughter [69] p103. Jeanne was also mistaken for the bride at Yvonne's wedding [70] p195.

Yvonne was accustomed to a lavish lifestyle whereas Joseph's finances were limited, but that was not a concern. Fernand presented the couple with a luxury Torpedo Type 156 Peugeot and pledged to pay the young family a life annuity of 12,000 francs a year.

After their wedding in early February, 1926, the pair moved to the Lariboisières district of Fontainebleau, where Joseph's artillery regiment was stationed. Yvonne was soon pregnant, giving birth to her son Freddy in Arles before the end of the same year.

Marie Blanc (?) and an Arlésienne, St. Trophime, 1926

In November 1926 a pair of women looking like Yvonne with Marie Blanc, director of the sewing school in La Roquette, appeared in a photograph of bishops led by Cardinal Charost at a mass celebrating the beatification of Jean Marie du Lau at St. Trophime.

However, Yvonne would have been in her 30th week of pregnancy at this time and there is no sign of a bump. It could be Jeanne or another woman standing on the steps, but they looked much alike.

Pregnancy can play havoc with the immune system and Yvonne fell ill. A photograph from April 1927 discovered by Patricia Couturier shows a group of ladies who had just completed a course of nursing.

Nursing course, Arles, 1927. Who is first on the left?

The man with the bow tie is Dr. Paul Béraud. He was their neighbour and Madame Calment recalled him well at the end of her life [65]. On the right is Joseph Imbert, then an intern and later a medic, mayor of Arles, and leader of the resistance during WWII. He died in a German prison camp in 1945. On the left at the front is a lady who again looks like Yvonne, but is she?

Yvonne   Arlésiens   Jeanne

Mme Calment reported that Yvonne had fallen ill by this time. We believe that in fact it is Jeanne who studied nursing to look after Yvonne, distinguished from her daughter in the photograph by her finer nose. Most of the other nurses in the picture are wearing a red cross to show that they are joining for general care of patients, but a few could have taken the course to look after someone in their own family. Perhaps Jeanne did not want to trust her daughter's care to another and was learning nursing skills to help look after Yvonne herself.

The next year in 1928, captain Billot applied for leave from army service. Joseph's disappointed superior said in a letter that

"His interests and the health of his wife obliged him to be in the proximity of Arles."

1928 letter on Billot's leave

By this time, Yvonne was seriously ill, and it would be clear to doctors that she was suffering from tuberculosis, a dangerous and stigmatized disease.

The pre-war records at Arles Hospital no longer exist and it is unlikely that Yvonne or Jeanne were ever treated there: patients who had tuberculosis usually preferred to keep this a secret and Calments could afford an expensive treatment outside of their hometown.

We don't know which doctors helped them after Dr. Urpar's death and Mme Calment had never talked about that. When Yvonne fell ill in 1927, her father Fernand was likely to seek a confidential advice from one of his acquaintances before sending her to a sanatorium.

In 1993 Mme Calment told her doctor Victor Lèbre (VL) that Yvonne was treated in the Savoy region:

[65] (25-26 February 1993, 18:40)	Translation
VL: Et vous vous rappelez quand elle a été malade, Yvonne ? MC: Oui. VL: Vous l'avez soigné chez vous? MC: <confused> Au début, et après... Après on a venu... au sana <sanatorium>. VL: C'était à quel	VL: And do you remember when she was sick, Yvonne? MC: Yes. VL: You treated her at home? MC: <confused> At first, and then... Afterwards we came... to the sana <sanatorium>.

endroit? MC: <confused> ah. mm. Ah. Haute Savoie. Ah m. Haute Savoie, je crois. Ah! VL: Vous vous rappelez à quel endroit? MC: <confused> Ah. mmm.. Je crois que Haute Savoie. VL: Elle y restait longtemps? MC: Pas tellement... C ´ est à la suite d'une pleurésie.	VL: Which place was that? MC: <confused> ah. mm. ah. Haute Savoy. Ah. m. Haute Savoie, I believe. Ah! VL: Which place, do you remember? MC: <confused> Ah. mmm.. I think Haute Savoy. VL: How long was she there? MC: Not so much... It was after a bout of pleurisy.

The Sanatorium Praz Coutant which opened on the plateau d'Assy in 1926 for the anti-tuberculosis crusade in France is the most likely place she would have gone to [71].

Sanatorium de Praz-Coutant

Luckily Yvonne did not have to stay there long. She had been fighting the infection in its latent extra-pulmonary form for a few years, so it was likely that her immune system was capable of resisting once it returned to normal strength after the pregnancy.

If any public rumours about Yvonne's health were circulating, they were soon quashed. In 1929 she posed at the steps of St. Trophime, for a photograph at the wedding of Joseph's brother Jean-Paul with Jeanne Guillet.

Jean-Paul

Joseph Yvonne

Jean Paul's wedding, 1929

Around the same time, she appeared at a costume festival. That photo was dated 1924 in the Arles Médiathèque (the library located in the former hospital

Hôtel Dieu). There was a dispute regarding the look of Yvonne on this photo but the daughter of her second cousin Pierre Fassin who owns a copy confirmed her identification.

François Robin-Champigneul had compared the picture with postcards from St. Trophime from various years and has shown that it was probably taken in 1930.

~1930, Cloître St. Trophime

This seems to contradict the official narrative as later told, according to which Yvonne was gravely ill and four years away from her funeral. Did the infection relapse again? While Yvonne was back to being seen in polite society in Arles, someone else was missing. Her mother Jeanne was not pictured or noted at any more events.

More than fifty years later Madame Calment entered the *Maison du Lac* retirement home and underwent routine medical examination including X-rays. The tests showed lungs scarred with pleural sequelae and bones so decalcified that, according to Dr. Levraud, they seemed almost transparent. She claimed never to have been ill, but her pleural sequelae might be signs of an earlier bout of tuberculosis [34].

Whether the elderly Mme Calment was Yvonne or Jeanne, the conclusion is the same. Jeanne Calment too had fallen victim to the prevalent disease of those times. She might have caught it while caring for Yvonne. As her daughter recovered and appeared back in public, Jeanne had to seek treatment.

We don't have details of every move they made during those troubled years. Jeanne might have been treated in more than one hospital. The census returns for the family in March 1931 are confused and unreliable. Yvonne was not recorded, and Jeanne's name appears to have been wrongly transcribed as Maria. Jeanne's father had died a few months before and her mother-in-law passed away soon after, leaving Fernand in sole charge of the shop.

At a time when Yvonne might have first encountered tuberculosis, the Calment family still had the means to be decadent. During the month of August 1916, as vast numbers of soldiers were dying in the battle of the Somme to the North, Mme Calment's name was recorded in *La Savoie Thermale* as resident at the *Grand Hotel des*

Baigneurs in Brides-les-Bains, a hedonistic spa town in the French Alps. There the bourgeoisie could sejour to lose weight while enjoying the high-class lifestyle in the casinos or on leisurely mountain walks.

By the beginning of the 1930s things were very different. The economy was in the grip of an inter-war depression which would hit the family's business hard. They had staff to pay and tried to keep the shop stocked with expensive and fashionable items. In 1928 Fernand bought a couple of adjacent buildings to open a furniture store.

It was bad timing. From 1929 until 1935 France suffered a rapid deflation. According to a local newspaper from May 1934, prices in Arles dropped by 26% in one year. Salaries for employees in the store were harder to bring down while firing them was not an option: they were good friends of Fernand. As fashions shifted from twenties to thirties, it would be all too easy for the Calments to find themselves lumbered with out-of-date items that might be difficult to sell at a good price.

If the store had a debt burden, then its finances would quickly deteriorate with deflation. In 1931 Fernand handled several sales of property that he, Jeanne and her brother François had inherited from their deceased parents. This helped the family keep the business solvent and pay for expensive tuberculosis treatment.

The Calment's world was in turmoil, but a photo of Yvonne that she sent out to friends and family gives a different impression. It shows her relaxed, dressed in highly fashionable baggy pants and carrying an oriental style parasol while posing on a hotel terrace in the Alps.

The photo appeared in French and British papers during the 1990s, without the background and mislabeled as a picture of the young Jeanne Calment on holiday. In 2019, an original dated August 1931 was unearthed.

Yvonne Calment in August 1931 in Leysin

In 2019 we identified the location of this photo after Nadine Lefevre from the counter-investigation group recognised the style of balcony as typical in Leysin, Switzerland, a resort where wealthy clients were being treated for tuberculosis. Rather than a picture from just a hotel it turned out to be at the Belvédère sanatorium there.

Leysin in 1946. Belvédère terrace and chalet Palettaz

It is our understanding that Yvonne was well at that time. She certainly looked it. That being the case, it is probable that she was there to visit Jeanne.

On 19th September 1931 it was reported in the press that Fernand attended a musical festival in Arles, but Jeanne was not mentioned while the wives of other guests were. Fernand could excuse her absence by the death of her father in the beginning of the year – she was still mourning.

Two months later in November 1931 Jeanne was back in Arles to sign off the sale of property she inherited from her father. This was done in the presence of the notary Victor Lucien Arnaud who knew the family well.

We obtained a copy of the signature which matched other documents from recent years, confirming that it was indeed Jeanne who signed. In early 1932 she did further paperwork related to her dowry money. Nevertheless, Jeanne was not making public appearances. She was probably still not well.

At the end of October Fernand resigned from the post of vice-president of the local entertaining club "Cercle de l'Avenir" where he had been a shareholder since 1904. At the same time, Joseph Billot was elected as a commissioner of this club.

The situation would have been particularly difficult for Freddy. In his earliest years his mother was ill with tuberculosis and separated from him to avoid contagion. At other times she was travelling with Joseph and did not pamper her son too much with her attention. It was not unusual for bourgeois families to employ a nanny to look after their young children. As Laure Meuzy, the head nurse in the retirement home who was believed to be the most intimate confidant of Mme Calment said about Yvonne,

> "A nurse had brought up the little one. Jeanne didn't want to have more children; she put her own life first." [72]

Freddy might have spent a lot of time with his grandmother Jeanne before she too became ill. According to Calment's biographers, he would want to call her *"maman"*, but they tried to get him to name her Jeanne. He settled for *"Manzane"*, a contraction of *"maman Jeanne"* [73] p77, [74] p129.

After Jeanne's illness isolated her from her grandson, he was probably looked after by his other grandmother, Marie Jouve, and his aunts and uncles Nenette Billot and Pierre Flauder, or with Jean-Paul Billot and Jeanne Guillet. Their children, Josette and Robert, were very close to Freddy in later years. Even when they lived in different towns they often travelled together in the Alps and met in Paradou.

Billot cousins, late 1930s

Jeanne wanted to keep her disease in secret. Rumours of Yvonne's health problems could be damaging back in 1928 but Jeanne's illness meant that the entire family of shopkeepers for the rich were afflicted with a deadly contagious disease of the poor. Maison Calment was struggling to keep afloat during the deflationary depression, and this could be the last blow for the business.

Yvonne's relapse, on the other hand, would have a much milder effect: she lived her own life since 1926, and some people already knew that she was ill in 1928. One member of a family could be struck by pleurisy and Jeanne blamed this on Maria exposing Yvonne to the cold waters of the Rhône on a hot day. If Jeanne were known to have a similar condition it would be harder to pretend it was not a contagious disease such as tuberculosis.

In Leysin it was known to doctors that Jeanne Calment was the patient, but not so in France. She returned to Arles in relatively good health in late 1931, but when she relapsed a year later, the family must have told local doctors that it was Yvonne who was ill again.

Jeanne's doctor, Maurice Gilbert, recommended his patients to stay at home with their families. She needed a place to be treated, but the farm Rouiron was not well suited for that purpose.

Fernand's business fortune was under strain and he was not fully protected from the debts of his store. Jeanne had her own money inherited from her parents while their marriage contract kept their finances separate. Moving some of their wealth to Jeanne would be prudent, but she was now seriously unwell and unable to meet the notary. In February 1933 a sunny villa was bought in a small village Paradou a few miles East of Arles.

The Calment's villa "La Miquelette" in Paradou

The purchase was signed in the name of Jeanne Calment, but this time her signature was different. The notary had also changed. Louis David had taken over the role from retired Arnaud. He came from outside Arles so probably did not know the Calment family as well as his predecessor. He would have been easily fooled if Yvonne signed in place of Jeanne. The changing signature is evidence that an identity switch had already taken place, a year before the funeral.

Initially, Yvonne had planned to revert the switch back when her mother recovered: she would have no need to ever meet this notary again after she extracted money from Jeanne's account and signed the purchase of the villa in 1933, securing the family finances.

Paradou is the Provençal name for the water mills used in the old days by the drapers who settled along the Arcoule river. Located close to the beautiful mountain range of the Alpilles, the ancient village was a paradise for its inhabitants. Van Gogh painted some of his best pictures in Saint-Rémy nearby and later the region became popular with French celebrities such as Charles Aznavour, Jean-Paul Belmondo and Brigitte Bardot.

With open galleries facing the same way as those at the Belvédère sanatorium in Leysin, the quietly situated and easily accessible villa named *"la Miquelette"* was a perfect place for continuing the heliotherapy widely used to cure tuberculosis before antibiotics became available.

After the funeral in 1934, la Miquelette would become a refuge for Mme Calment where she could start a new life, avoiding unwanted encounters with fellow Arlesians for the next few years. It was her favourite home until 1963.

[65] (6 and 13 July 1994, 03:26)	Translation
VL: Vous vous rappelez votre maison de campagne du Paradou? MC: Bah! Quelle question?! VL: Elle s'appelait comment? MC: La Miquelette. VL: C'est vous qui	VL: Do you remember your country house in Paradou? MC: What a question! VL: What was it called? MC: La Miquelette. VL: Did you name it that? MC: No, yeah, that's what

l'aviez baptisé comme ça?

MC: No, ouais, c'est que c'est comme ça. C'était son nom.

VL: C'est une maison où vous alliez l'été?

MC: Oui. L'été, l'hiver. L'hiver agréable.

VL: Qu'est-ce que vous faisait là-bas? Vous preniez les repas dehors l'été?

MC: Non, surtout.

VL: Vous prenez toujours les repas. Il n'y avait pas de d'ombrage?

MC: Pas l'été.

VL: Vous preniez vos repas dedans?

MC: Une grande salle à manger, fraîches, belle, maison moderne.

VL: Vous l'aviez meublé avec des meubles modernes?

MC: Comment?

VL: Vous, vous aviez des meubles modernes pour l'époque?

it is. That was its name.

VL: It's a house where you used to go in the summer?

MC: Yes. Summer, winter. Nice winter.

VL: What were you doing there? Did you eat outside in the summer?

MC: No, mostly.

VL: You always had meals... there was no shade?

MC: Not in the summer.

VL: Did you take your meals inside?

MC: A big dining room, cool, beautiful, modern house.

VL: Did you furnish it with modern furniture?

MC: What?

VL: Did you have modern furniture for that time?

MC: No, antique furniture.

VL: It was family furniture?

MC: Yes.

VL: How many rooms

MC: Non, des meubles anciens.
VL: C'étaient des meubles de famille?
MC: Oui.
VL: Il y avait combien de pièces à cette Miquelette?
MC: Bah, il y avait trois chambres, salon et salle à manger, et une cuisine...
VL: Vous ne mangiez pas à la cuisine?
MC: Non.
VL: Vous aviez la bonne avec vous?
MC: Oui.
VL: Vous y alliez avec Yvonne et avec Frédéric?
MC: Oui.
VL: C'est là que vous faisait de la bicyclette?
MC: Oui.

were there in this Miquelette?
MC: Well, there were three bedrooms, living room and dining room, and a kitchen...
VL: Didn't you eat in the kitchen?

MC: No.
VL: Did you have the maid with you?
MC: Yes.
VL: Did you go there with Yvonne and with Frédéric?
MC: Yes.
VL: Is that where you used to ride your bicycle?
MC: Yes.

They may have moved furniture from Calment's appartments in Arles to the villa, replacing it with hard to sell items from the shop.

For at least some of the time Yvonne was masquerading as Jeanne who must have been too unwell to make an appearance and was treated at Paradou as her daughter by the doctor and nurses who hadn't known them earlier.

When Jeanne returned to Arles for Christmas 1933, she would be very ill [73] p77, [74] p76. Her loss of weight would make her unrecognisable. The priests, doctors, servants, and relatives would easily believe she was Yvonne. Yvonne would also have an opportunity to test whether she could pass herself off as Jeanne. By that time, they had been out of the public eye for a while, but could she really get away with such an audacious scam?

We believe that Yvonne had early onset of greying hair. She had used dark hair dye in the Leysin photo, but if she washed out the colour, she would immediately appear older. Even with darker hair, mother and daughter could easily be confused. Never working, they had spent much of their time together so they would have had very similar voices and mannerisms. It is known that they were mistaken for each other, not only by validators and journalists, but also by some of the guests at Yvonne's wedding [69]. Only close family and friends would see through the ruse.

Yvonne

Jeanne

Yvonne knew that by posing as Jeanne she would put an end to harmful rumours about her illness, but there was another reason why deception was necessary at this time.

Joseph, who was by then well integrated into the family and using the double name Billot-Calment, was nearing the end of his 5-year leave of absence from the army. His help was desperately needed to look after secretly ill Jeanne, small Freddy, and Fernand's store. Jeanne was treated and Yvonne was hiding in their villa, so Joseph's ability to drive the car was indispensable for their moves from Paradou to Arles and back.

He could only get an extension of leave if his own wife was still ill, so pretending that it was Yvonne rather than Jeanne who was suffering from tuberculosis was too good a trick to miss. Joseph's leave was renewed for another 5 years in 1933.

Initially they expected that Jeanne would recover, and with necessary precautions such as avoiding the doctor, notary, and other witnesses, everything could gradually return to normal with nobody outside their close circle being aware of what happened. It seemed like an honest fraud, a white lie, harming nobody. Yvonne took on the role of Jeanne with growing confidence, amused at her ability to take in even her Calment cousins with the deception.

The lie began innocently but grew out of control: when circumstances do not progress as planned it becomes necessary to invent increasingly bigger lies to cover smaller ones. When four-year-old Freddy started calling Yvonne *Manzane* on her return from Leysin, as he had called Jeanne before her illness, the children of the staff at the shop he was playing with at the time might decide that she was Jeanne. This helped to create the impression that Jeanne was well, and Yvonne began to pass herself off as her mother to strangers. Later they needed Freddy to fully accept that Manzane was his grandmother, otherwise he might have blabbed about the switch.

It seems like a callous act of deception, but they had committed signature fraud and lied to Joseph's superiors about why he was on leave. The consequences of not maintaining the switch could be scandalous for the family. She hoped that after Jeanne's recovery they would travel away for some time and then swap back, tricking little Freddy again.

As Jeanne's health worsened, the Calments were faced with a terrible problem. They hoped Jeanne would recover but when she died, they were in too deep. Many people were already convinced that it was Yvonne who was ill. The death was registered by the doctor and other witnesses as the death of Yvonne. At that point the family had no easy way out. They faced the choice of confessing to her misdeeds or making the identity swap permanent.

The admission would be too disastrous. Signature fraud is a very serious matter and there was a risk of a breaking scandal far worse than the one they had originally tried to avoid. Yvonne could face criminal proceedings and Joseph might be court-marshalled for his deception to obtain leave.

Desperate circumstances required desperate measures and now they had no other option but to continue the pretence by telling all those relatives who were not complicit, including Freddy, that it was Yvonne who had died. Emotionally Freddy would not feel that the deceased was his true mother, but childhood amnesia would fade any residual memory of who she really was. Yvonne would have to become *Manzane* and continue the masquerade indefinitely.

Zak originally proposed a purely financial reason for the identity switch [24]. On Jeanne's death the Calments would have inheritance tax to pay on her property that they could barely afford under the harsh economic circumstances. This motive still holds but it was not strong enough on its own for Yvonne to give up her own identity and risk the legal consequences of the fraud.

It is now clear that the non-financial pressures they were under would be the greater driving force behind their actions: the identity switch had already taken place by 1933 when Jeanne's presence was needed to sign documents and they tried to hide her illness. Faking Yvonne's relapse was safer for the shop's reputation and allowed Joseph's leave from the army to be extended.

Paradoxically, the main driving force behind the final identity switch after Jeanne's death in 1934 was not the financial gain, but the fear of being exposed.

There is another element of Yvonne's motive which is less concrete, but it should not be ignored – her sense of guilt. If Jeanne had caught tuberculosis from Yvonne as we suspect, it would be a heavy burden for her conscience to bear. She wished that she could turn back time and put it right. She would be willing to sacrifice her own life to bring back her mother. By switching identity, that is what she did, at least in the minds of those who believed (and still believe) that Jeanne Calment did not die in 1934.

Before the switch, Yvonne hardly ever smiled in photographs, whereas after 1934, Mme Calment is usually seen cheering and laughing. When asked how she would like to live her life if she had to do it over again, she confidently said

"The same! I have had a good life, a wonderful life!" [65] (15 June 1995 02:25)

After the switch, Yvonne has got a new destiny – to preserve the secret. She embraced the adventure she lacked before. Her long-held dream of becoming famous had finally come true. Madame Calment was clearly proud of her achievement – to fool the whole town and then the whole world.

AFTERLIFE

Like Einstein is a symbol of intelligence, Rockefeller of wealth, Mozart of music and Cleopatra of beauty, the name Calment is a symbol of longevity.

M. Allard and J.-M. Robine [1]

J eanne passed away on 19th January 1934 on Yvonne's 36th birthday at 2 a.m. Extreme unction was given by Abbé Paul Lacroux (1883-1947), curate at St. Trophime, at Jeanne's bedside. She died of respiratory failure, unable to speak. The vicar smeared oil on her forehead and laid his hands on her, reciting a prayer for Yvonne's soul.

Catholics believe that all sins except blasphemy against the Holy Spirit will be forgiven provided there is repentance. Yvonne did not want to do wrong, but there was also a duty to protect her family. She must have convinced herself that her actions were the lesser evil.

"I knew all the pleasures plus one" and *"I had all the vices and one more,"* [75]

said Mme Calment at the end of her life, and added that she was a believer *in her own way*. She was seen in church frequently after the passing of all her family in 1963, but much less is known about the times when she was younger. Her religiosity has fluctuated over time:

> *"Until now I have been very religious. Now I'm floating, I'm undecided. Is there really a God who lets all these wars happen? Mind you, I still say my prayers and thank him every night because I don't suffer from anything."* [61, 76]

Abbé Paul Lacroux at St. Trophime

In the morning of 20th January, the Calments invited people to come at 15-00 to the house of the deceased at rue Gambetta. Yvonne's death was announced on behalf of an impressively long list of people. Some lived away from Arles, others avoided close contact with Calments for a while out of fear of becoming infected. They already believed that it was Yvonne who was ill and probably had to be fooled again.

Le Capitaine BILLOT-CALMENT, Chevalier de la Légion d'honneur, Croix de Guerre ;
Monsieur Frédéric BILLOT-CALMENT ;
Monsieur et Madame Fernand CALMENT ;
Madame Veuve Paul BILLOT ;
Madame Veuve ESPEYTE et sa fille ;
Monsieur et Madame Albert BILLOT et leurs enfants, de St-Rambert-d'Albon;
Monsieur et Madame Paul BILLOT et leur fils, de Lyon ;
Monsieur et Madame Pierre FLAUDER et leur fille ;
Monsieur et Madame François CALMENT, de Toulon ;
Mademoiselle Elisa FELIX ;
Monsieur et Madame Auguste JAMBON ;
Madame Veuve JOUVE, de Carpentras ;
Monsieur et Madame FEJOZ et leur fille, de Carpentras ;
Monsieur et Madame François JOUVE et leur fille, d'Alès ;
Monsieur et Madame Prosper JOUVE, de Marseille ;
Monsieur et Madame Nicolas CROUANSON et leurs enfants ;
Mademoiselle Marthe FASSIN ;
Monsieur et Madame Théodore FASSIN, avocat ;
Monsieur et Madame Léon FASSIN ;
Monsieur et Madame MICHEL et leurs enfants, de Marseille ;
Le Capitaine et Madame Albert MANARANCHE, et leurs enfants, de Marseille;
Mademoiselle Marguerite MINAUD ;
Le Personnel de la Maison CALMENT ;
Les familles CALMENT, CABASSUT, LAVANDET, SIBBONS, LEBAS, ROUSSEAU, BOURDELON, BOUJON, MARION, FABRE, PETIT, TROUCHE, PELOUX,
Ont la douleur de vous faire part de la perte cruelle qu'ils viennent d'éprouver en la personne de

Madame Yvonne BILLOT-CALMENT

leur épouse, mère, fille, belle-fille, belle-sœur, tante, nièce, cousine, amie et alliée, décédée le 19 Janvier 1934, à l'âge de 36 ans, munie des sacrements de l'église.

Et vous prient de vouloir bien assister à ses obsèques qui auront lieu le Samedi 20 Janvier 1934, à 15 heures, en l'église Primatiale Saint-Trophime.

On se réunira à la maison mortuaire : rue Gambetta.

Priez pour Elle!

Invitation to the funeral

It should be noted that such standard notices are not a good indication of close observance. In 1937 Mme Calment was included in a similar announcement on the death of Paul Crouanson, son of Fernand's cousin and close friend Nicolas Crouanson. However, in a conversation with her doctor, Mme Calment said that she had not followed the Crouanson's boys, and couldn't even recall their names [65] (23 June 1994 6:45). This shows how distant she became even from her closest relatives.

Some of the people mentioned on the card were complicit, probably including most Billots and Marguerite Minaud, the cousin of Jeanne's mother that had served as the family's live-in domestic help when Jeanne was a child.

The funeral was the day after the passing so there was not much time for visitors to see the body. It was Saturday and many people, including doctors, politicians and the like would be in the country and miss the ceremony which was announced in the morning and started at 3pm. There would also be limited opportunity for relatives from other towns to make the journey.

The note invited people to gather at the house of the deceased, rue Gambetta, but it didn't say that there will be a viewing of the body. Most guests were supposed to meet near the store and walk with the cortège to the funeral.

J. Arnaud's obituary

Yvonne's obituary

J. Granaud's funeral, Arles, 27.02.1934

1935 mass
AVIS MORTUAIRES

Saturday is a big market day in Arles and people could join the procession after the market was closed. The local newspaper reported that despite the rainy weather a large crowd came out to accompany the deceased to her final resting place and pay their respects, but this does not mean they would be aware of a switch.

An equally large crowd had already gathered there earlier that week for another funeral related to Maison Calment: Jérôme Arnaud, a prominent employee of the shop for some 40 years, died the previous Saturday and was buried two days later.

In the months leading up to her death in 1934 Jeanne would be in a very weak state: she was probably wasted by tuberculosis. This would make it even harder for doctors and funeral directors to judge her age. They had no reason to be suspicious of a switch, especially since they knew that Yvonne had been ill a few years before.

We don't know for certain if the body was on view for the funeral, but if it was then it could have been treated with embalming fluid to make her look more normal. The family only had to give the undertakers Yvonne's photo and clothes and they would apply makeup so that she would have a right look, without knowing that they were party to a deception.

Yvonne herself had ceased to dye her hair so that it turned grey making her look older. She was similar enough to Jeanne that a change of dress, hairstyle and make-up would be sufficient. As people paid their last respects, Mme Calment would sit by with a veil over her face. With Yvonne's bold and cold-blooded nature, the trickery would be easy to pass off.

In January 1935 the family announced that a mass in Yvonne's memory would be held in the strictest privacy. The months and even years after the funeral they would be in mourning. Mme Calment had gone to Paradou, broken by grief, and devoted herself to Freddy. By that time, she lost connections with most of her friends and relatives with some notable exceptions like Antoinette and Jean-Paul Billot.

On rare occasions when she was seen in Arles, Yvonne's growing resemblance to her late mother allowed her to easily pass herself off as Jeanne. Only her closest friends and relatives would have an opportunity to notice the switch and they were complicit.

Joseph was now working in the store and participated in the military drills. Fernand has restricted his social activity due to the deep mourning. He avoided such events like the ball on May 8, 1934, of the association of the former students at the College of Arles where he was a president for many years. From July to September, Fernand lived alone in the Hotel des Bains in Uriage, a resort he enjoyed visiting with his wife when they were younger.

Three years later, Fernand did not accompany Mme Calment on her trip to Paris. She was photographed in Versailles in 1937 with Freddy and the family of his uncle Jean-Paul Billot. Joseph would likely have taken the photo.

Billots in Versailles, 1937

Billots in Paris, 1937

Unfortunately, Mme Calment is missing on another picture of the family reunion in Paris, perhaps this time she was the photographer.

While at least some of Joseph's siblings were in on the switch, their children were kept in the dark. Most of the Calment side of the family were also unaware, except for Fernand and Jeanne's brother François who lived in Toulon.

When Yvonne was not travelling, she stayed mostly in her villa in Paradou. Freddy was taken to school in Arles where he did very well. When seen in the town, his grandmother was usually wearing a veil and snubbing those who looked at her too closely [72].

Maison Calment struggled to adapt to the new economic

environment. Fernand took a 150,000FF loan from a bank in 1935 backing it by his property and sold a villa in Saint Maries de la Mer in 1937. In 1938, four years after the funeral, Joseph was called back to the army and the family business was shut down.

Fernand avoided bankruptcy by doing a deal with a competitor store Maison Bouisson, renting out the premises at a deflation-proof rate fixed for ten years that covered payments on outstanding debts. By that time, the economy was suffering from inflation rather than the deflation of the previous years, so the fixed rent was a better deal for the Bouisson side.

It was then that Mme Calment developed one of her favourite pastimes – hunting rabbits, wild boar, and partridges with her Jack Russel terrier and 18mm rifle.

"It was said that it would mess up your hair and damage your skin. Did you see that? I haven't got a wrinkle." [75]

Madame Calment in 1943, Paradou

In June 1940 Joseph played a notable role in the defence of the Maginot Line near Épinal just before the capitulation of France. It was believed that he was captured there on the day of armistice and taken as a prisoner of war, but it is more likely that he escaped the advancing Germans and went on to fight in Syria before the return to his hometown in 1941. There he urged his compatriots to collaborate with Marshal Pétain.

In 1942, shortly before the German occupation of Arles, Joseph became an Officer of the Legion of Honour and Fernand died. Mme Calment said that it was liver disease provoked by copper sulphate on cherries. The remaining family thrived during the occupation, the Allied bombings of 1944, and the liberation.

After the hostilities, Joseph retired and sold his share in the Billot family house to his niece Josette. Freddy went to medical school where he met dental student Renée Taque. They married in Paradou in 1950 and settled above the space of the former Calment shop in Arles, next door to Mme Calment who shared the adjacent apartment with her official son-in-law.

The Mas de Rouiron was sold, and some was used to set up Renée's dental practice at their address in Arles. This was a generous gift from Mme Calment. It might also be seen as a settlement of money owed in accordance with dowry commitments in the marriage contract of Yvonne and Joseph.

La Miquelette in 1950s

Joseph Billot and Mme Calment, ~1960

Mme Calment was able to live some good years with her family, always playing the part of Jeanne. Her run of tragedy continued in 1963 when Joseph died of diabetes and Freddy had a fatal car accident.

Renée and Freddy did not have any children and it has been said that the marriage was not a happy one [77] p221, but it was Freddy's will to leave all his assets to Renée (Mme Calment did receive her minimum share guaranteed by law). After his death, the heirs organised a series of transactions under which Taque would try to accumulate Calment's former wealth including the villa in Paradou.

A part of this became an apocryphal story according to which Mme Calment entered into a *viager* deal with notary André-François Raffray in 1965. Raffray would pay a monthly sum of 2,500 Francs in return for possession of Jeanne's apartment after her death. Some of these reported details were not correct.

Our research of financial and legal documents found that from 1963 Mme Calment had a *viager* agreement with Taque that was partially covered by an annuity paid on the life of Madame Calment by the state assurance company CNP.

Several years later, the villa was returned, and the annuity was increased after a legal process instigated by Calment. Raffray, who was helping Taque sort out the financial problems that had fallen upon her, became involved in 1969 when he took over this additional viager part of the arrangement.

Both Raffray and the CNP got a raw deal: Mme Calment lived for another three decades instead of the few years that were expected for a woman already in her 90s.

On 21st February 1975 Jeanne Calment would be 100 years old. The mayor Jacques Perrot was aware of the anniversary and proposed a meeting. Mme Calment at first refused because he was a communist, but later she relented and went to see him. She appeared surprisingly young and healthy for her age and the mayor initially took her for her daughter [78].

Mme Calment mourned Freddy's death for the rest of her life and frequented his grave even after her move to the nursing home. In 2019, to prove the authenticity of Jeanne, Freddy's goddaughter Claudie Taque made public the letter to her mother Andrée Taque from 1977:

"Dear Dede, it was with pleasure that I read your letter. I have not heard from you for so long; I am very sensitive to your memory of my Freddy! This time is painful for me; oh, I do not need this to think of him; I continue to worship his memory every day; when we say that sorrow does not kill, it is very true; I imagine that despite my pain, I reached 102 1/2 years without anything being changed in any way; of course, I am not getting any better, but life goes on!

It's been 14 years since I buried the son and the father. Whose turn is when? You never know which surprises the future holds. If my Freddy knew everything that had happened since he left, what a pain; it wouldn't have happened... You know what I mean.

I hope you will give me news from time to time; I give you all a big hug; big kiss on the buttocks.

Ta mamé"

Mme Calment lived at home looking after herself until the age of 110 despite a steep staircase that she had to climb to reach her apartment. To avoid going out with a bucket to fetch water from the well, she accidentally started a small fire trying to unfreeze pipes and it was this that led to her being admitted to a retirement home, La Maison du Lac.

There she asked Nenette Billot's daughter Josette to burn

her photographs and other documents she left at home. Luckily, Josette decided to preserve some of them [69] p65.

Lifelong friendship

In 1986 Mme Calment achieved fame as she took the title of France's oldest living person. Her notoriety was amplified globally when she told a story that she had met Vincent Van Gogh in Arles in 1888. According to her account, she had been introduced to the artist by her husband Fernand when he visited their shop to buy canvases. After the centenary of Van Gogh's arrival at Arles was commemorated in 1988, Mme Calment got the role of Jeanne Calment in a Canadian docudrama about the artist. Later many questions over the consistency of this story were raised.

Arlesians knew Mme Calment to be a difficult character, *"une peste"*. At the retirement home the supercentenarian treated her carers as servants to do her bidding, earning her the nickname *"Commandant j'ordonne"* *(Commander I give orders)* [79]. When asked by a schoolchild how she washed the dishes she snapped back

> *"With spit my dear; I just needed to command."* [73] p15.

She drank port, ate chocolate in abundance and smoked expensive cigarettes, habits that were remnants of a well-healed past.

By 1995 at least five books about the Doyenne of humanity were being released. On 21 February she had received thousands of letters from all over the world.

> *"Calment lunched on crab, duck and champagne with friends at her retirement home before sharing a mammoth chocolate birthday cake with 80 guests, including France's health minister."* [80]

Her birthdays took on the proportions of national celebrations, bringing great joy to the old lady:

> *"I enjoy everything about it, I enjoy it all a lot. A bit more than a lot, perhaps."* [81]

After Raffray's died in 1995, his first and second wives continued to pay the annuity to Mme Calment for two years until she has set the unbeatable record of human lifespan of 122 years and 164 days.

Mme Calment was idolized by demographers, gerontologists, and the general public. Her validators had proudly stated that

> "*Like Einstein is a symbol of intelligence, Rockefeller of wealth, Mozart of music and Cleopatra of beauty, the name Calment is a symbol of longevity.*" [1]

Since then, a rare book, talk, or article in the field fails to admire her celebrated achievement in the most competitive of all sports, but was Madame Calment being honest?

THE POWER
OF LIES

Jeanne Calment's word and the extensive documentary detective work by Robine and Allard are the best we can rely on.

Tom Kirkwood [82]

T he head nurse in Maison du Lac and a good friend of Mme Calment in her late life, Laure Meuzy dismissed the identity switch because her experience in psychiatry suggested that

"It is impossible to play such a comedy for sixty years." [83]

In the beginning of 2019 Michel Allard and Jean-Marie Robin acknowledged the theoretical possibility of a switch, but with one delicate condition:

"I still think there was no substitution. But if that's

wrong and it was her daughter in front of us all these years, she was an exceptional liar." [84]

"If we accept their claims then she was not a champion of the world in longevity but a champion of the world in manipulation and intelligence!" [85]

Our assessment from 15 hours of audio recordings of her interviews [65] (see the following volume) is that Mme Calment was not an exceptionally good liar. She made many slips of identity and errors of consistency, and she was continually evasive, especially about details of her life before marriage. Her lie seems like a castle built of sand, so what could hold it together so tightly?

Being a successful liar is however not about weaving good lies. It is about building confidence and sympathy, so that people trust you no matter what you say. The best way to achieve that for Mme Calment was to persuade people that others already believed her. This started by convincing complicit friends and relatives to corroborate the lies, and by obtaining official documents such as an ID card and death certificate.

Officials are much less efficient at checking authenticity than should be expected, especially when there is no apparent reason to doubt it and the claimant is respectable.

We often hear that Mme Calment's claim must be true because so many people could not be wrong. First it was the doctors and notaries, then her neighbours and relatives, then the people of Arles and later the whole world. Many people can be fooled if they all believe each other.

We can argue that it is not Mme Calment who was an extraordinary liar, but it was her lie which enslaved her, grew up and became exceptionally powerful. Initially being small and innocent, it has gradually progressed into subjugating its victims. Among them were those who knew the truth but were obliged by circumstances to stick to the lie. These were Yvonne herself, her parents and husband, and very few close relatives.

There were also those who had initially no reason to distrust the lie, and after believing it had become resistant to admitting that they were fooled. Most people who looked after Mme Calment in the nursing home did not question her claim and ridiculed the rumours of her being Yvonne.

Doctor Lèbre was surprised by her mistakes and slips, but preferred to explain them away by assuming an unusual age-related combination of the lucidity with delirium. Finally, her validators believed her too, despite the many errors she made that should have alerted them to the truth. Their favourite argument was that they did not think so many other people could have been tricked.

It is easy to deceive those who want to be deceived. They achieved fame and success thanks to their believing in the lie and it became their vital interest to convince the rest. After the verification was complete, their colleagues, even those who were sceptics initially, declared this study an impeccable standard for age validation and admitted Calment's unquestionable authenticity.

The lie became too big to fail. By 1997, Jeanne Calment

was a national legend, President Chirac called her "everyone's grandmother" and the French State decided not to investigate her identity when insurance company officials raised doubts that she was in fact Yvonne [86].

Renowned gerontologist Tom Kirkwood finalized the marginalization of the possibility of identity switch by declaring that

> *"We should banish such thoughts from our minds. No witnesses to her earlier life are available, and no one is likely to exhume her and her relatives for DNA tests to confirm their relationships. She had lost all of her teeth long before her death, so dental records could be no help. Jeanne Calment's word and the extensive documentary detective work by Robine and Allard are the best we can rely on."* [82]

In 2019 it seemed that the lie had been exposed, but it has attracted new supporters and was successfully defended again by the original validators. Allard has proudly praised these efforts:

[87]	Translation
Une armée de détectives amateurs, surtout arlésiens, de journalistes d'investigation, de généalogistes et d'historiens est venue, dans un élan patriotique, compléter le dossier avec des milliers de	An army of amateur detectives, especially from Arles, investigative journalists, genealogists, and historians came, in a patriotic impulse, to complete the file

documents, de photos, d'articles, d'analyses, tous renforçant considérablement la véracité de l'âge de JLCC. Ainsi, malgré elle, JLCC <Madame Jeanne Louise Calment Calment> mis, une fois de plus, la barre très haut (un peu à la manière de Bubka) pour ce qui est de la validation de son âge.	with thousands of documents, photos, articles, analyses, all greatly reinforcing the veracity of Calment's age. Thus, JLCC < Madame Jeanne Louise Calment Calment > sets, once again, the bar very high (a bit like Bubka) for what is about validating her age.

Neither the validators nor most of their supporters had ever declared any other goal than "to prove" what they already "knew". They proclaimed loudly that the new facts confirmed that they were right [38] and celebrated the victory. Those scientists who supported exhumation were silenced and the press reported that the Tarascon court had closed the case without opening it.

Science is supposed to be self-correcting.

> *"A spirit of rebellion is absolutely necessary to be able to follow your scientific intuition despite the accepted views."* [20]

When the evidence is not solid, someone will eventually question it and analyse the claim without being swayed by the authority of other experts. This has happened many times before. At some point the claim of the flatness of the Earth was questioned despite almost everybody living on this planet believing it to be flat. It is this spirit of rebellion and search for truth that encouraged us to examine the testimony and documentary evidence in the case of Mme Calment's claimed longevity.

People are used to basing their opinion on the position of the expert community. Unfortunately, the Jeanne Calment's identity switch hypothesis runs counter to the interests of any of the recognised expert groups on the subject. Not only professional gerontologists and demographers, but also amateur validators who are busy verifying longevity claims are very much opposed to anyone questioning Calment, the universally recognised benchmark for age validation. If this record is fake then all their work for other supercentenarians that was based on official documents and newspaper articles would also be questioned.

Because of the enormous universal confidence in her authenticity, we have had to go to extraordinary lengths to gather information over a period of four years. We ask only that the direct evidence from this multivolume book is considered on its own merits and not on what has been said by those who had less complete facts to go on.

It takes time and effort to get to the bottom of this issue. It is more difficult than assuming that neither side of the Calment debate can ever prove its case without DNA testing, but we are sure that the patient reader will get the satisfaction of knowing that the truth exists, and it is cognisable.

The story of Calment's longevity record is an excellent example of the power of lies but it is not at all unique. Humans are very vulnerable to deception and scientists are not immune to this vulnerability. To avoid being enslaved by lies it is important to understand their danger.

SIGNATURES

This reminds me of 'NASA stages the moon landing.'
And someone besides Lee Harvey Oswald shot Kennedy.
Which is that people are looking for tiny inconsistencies
in evidence that probably have no meaning and then
overlooking a vast amount of evidence that her identity
is confirmed with more than 30 government documents.

Steven Austad [29]

J eanne Calment was required to sign many documents during her life. When people sign their name, they typically use stylised script, different from their normal handwriting, to make it distinct.

Over time a signature can evolve. Nonetheless, if Jeanne underwent an identity switch at an age of almost sixty years, any sudden change should stand out. This provides an excellent means to not only check whether the switch took place, but also to narrow down when it happened.

Luckily a good number of examples of her signature on official documents have been preserved. Until recently we had only one from the period between 1928 and 1946 and its exact date was uncertain. Now we have obtained five more documents signed during the crucial years from 1931 to 1933. Below are twenty-two samples we found, in chronological order.

Jeanne's early signatures, written between 1896 and 1900, feature her full first name. The most noticeable evolution during this time is the addition of an underlining tail back from the final "t".

	Marriage contract, 7 Apr 1896
	Marriage, 8 Apr 1896
	Marriage, 8 Apr 1896
	Marriage of Marguerite Crouanson, 14 Apr 1898

| 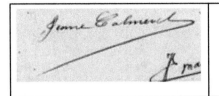 | Marriage of Marthe Calment, 5 Jun 1900 |

By 1924 Jeanne's signature had evolved further. Only the first initial "J" was used for her given name, and the "C" of the family name had a tail instead of a curl. Other features including the tail on the "t" remained.

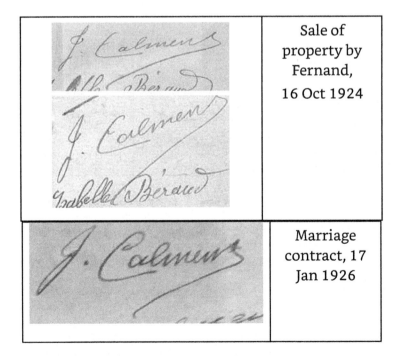

| | Sale of property by Fernand, 16 Oct 1924 |
| | Marriage contract, 17 Jan 1926 |

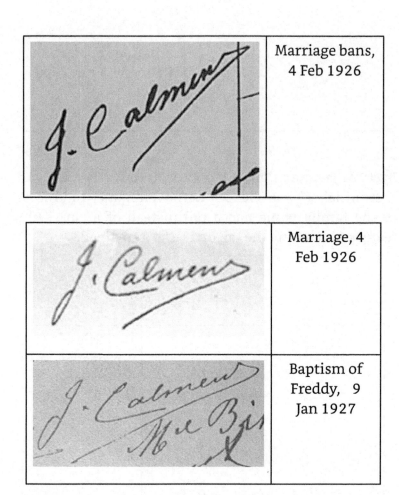

	Marriage bans, 4 Feb 1926
	Marriage, 4 Feb 1926
	Baptism of Freddy, 9 Jan 1927

This much change over 24 years is not surprising. Although the signature varies slightly from one example to another, it remained stable over the ten samples available from 1924 until early 1932.

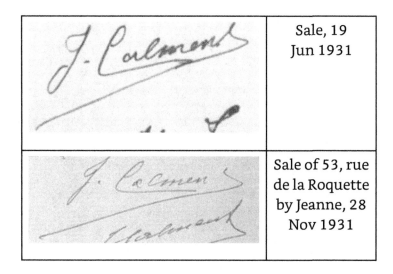

	Sale, 19 Jun 1931
	Sale of 53, rue de la Roquette by Jeanne, 28 Nov 1931

The February 1932 autograph is not unlike the previous ones, but something dramatic seems to have happened in the 1933 documents. Jeanne suddenly reverts to using her full first name and the tail on the "t" vanishes. In many ways she seems to have returned to the style she used on her marriage contract 35 years earlier, except that the tail on the "C" is retained.

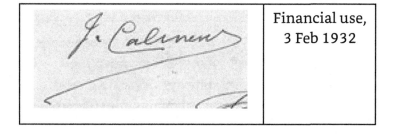

	Financial use, 3 Feb 1932

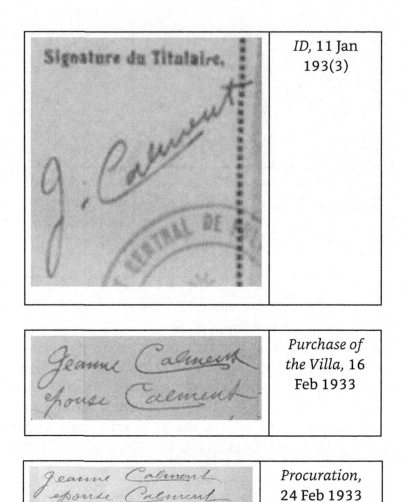

	ID, 11 Jan 193(3)
	Purchase of the Villa, 16 Feb 1933
	Procuration, 24 Feb 1933

After 1933 she goes back to just the initial "*J*", but the new signature is noticeably different from the way it looked during 1924 to 1932. The loop of the letter "*J*" is rounder showing that it is now drawn in one continuous stroke instead of two. In the earlier signatures the pen reversed direction at the top, although the way this was done varied with loops or cusps.

	Tax asset declaration 6 Jul 1946
	Letter, 1957
	Letter, 1977

	Letter, 1984

The missing tail on the "*t*" is the most striking difference that stands out in all of the signatures after 1932. Also, the "*l*" is higher on the ID card and some later cases, a feature never seen earlier. The rest of the letters in the usual hand script of the time look much the same. She continued to use this style of signature for decades after.

A direct comparison of the differences shows a clear *switch* in 1933.

1924-1933	1933-1984	1924-33	1933-1984

Switch in "J"   Switch in "t"

Why did it change so markedly between February 1932 and February 1933? Jeanne was 57 years old, and her signature has been stable for the previous ten and following fifty years. Some evolution might be expected over time but not a major adjustment in the space of just

12 months.

One thing we know is that the notary they used to write their legal documents had also changed. Previously Victor Lucien Arnaud had handled all their notarial work. His signature appeared under the purchase of the Maison Calment by Jacques from his grandmother-in-law in 1881; he had written the marriage contract for Jeanne and Fernand in 1896, and again for Yvonne and Joseph in 1926. He continued to work with the Calments for more than half a century up until 1932. He would have known the family very well by that time.

On the 24 June 1932 Arnaud retired at the age of 77 and his position was taken over by Louis David, a young notary from Grenoble who had relocated to Arles. David met the Calments to draw up their next legal transaction which appears to have been the purchase of the family villa in Paradou in 1933.

To ensure that all legal matters were handled as required the notary would need to refer to the marriage contract of Jeanne and Fernand from 1896. He would probably show this to the couple to make sure they understood their complex financial obligations to each other. The signature Mme Calment used in 1933 seemed to partly reflect the form she had written on the marriage contract.

Nevertheless, there is no reason why Jeanne should have changed her signature to match the earlier document. If necessary, she could show David more recent samples. Nor is it clear why her signature should not have reverted to its earlier form in later documents, for example, in casual letters of no legal significance.

A more plausible explanation considering the possibility

that there was an identity switch, is that it happened between February 1932 and February 1933. The change in notary means that when Yvonne took over the identity of her mother and forged her signature, it could go unnoticed that she was a different person.

We are not aware of all the details of what transpired, but the first forged signature we know is probably the one on an identity card issued in Jeanne's name. Perhaps Yvonne had to do it in a hurry and from memory without reference to a sample, which is why it is so different from Jeanne's previous signatures.

The next changed signatures are on the purchase documents for the villa a few weeks later. They appear to have a lot in common with the autograph on the marriage contract from 1896, so perhaps Yvonne was trying to check against this old sample while forging her signature in front of the notary.

After this deal, Madame Calment never again reverted to the style used by Jeanne before.

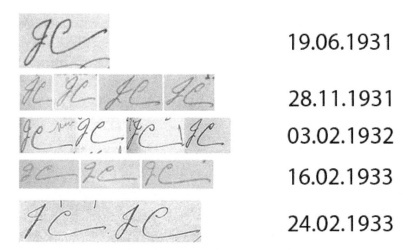

19.06.1931

28.11.1931

03.02.1932

16.02.1933

24.02.1933

Margin initials

In addition to the final signatures on the documents there are initials *"JC"* seen in the margins. These are used by the signatories to acknowledge a change or addition.

Here the *"J"* varies between pointed and rounded. As with the handwriting, the initials can be different from the full signature. We therefore assume that Jeanne and Yvonne used both variants of the *"J"* in their handwriting. However, the difference between the initials from 16 and 24 February 1933 is still striking.perhaps Yvonne, who originally had a coarser handwriting, was still in the process of developing her new style, or the latter signature was done at home by Jeanne herself.

Anyway, for the signature, Jeanne always used the pointed *"J"* before 1933, whereas after 1933 Mme Calment used the rounded *"J"*.

The change in signature is one of the strongest single

pieces of evidence in favour of the identity switch. As we noted in our older Bayesian analysis in 2019 [48], it is also a strong motive for faking Yvonne's death in place of Jeanne's. Signature fraud is a serious crime making it very difficult for them to undo the identity switch when Jeanne died.

Since our earlier analysis, this evidence has gained strength. The new finds narrow the gap between different signatures of known date from seven years to only the 12 months after February 1932. This is now a period much too short for natural evolution from one hand to explain the drastic transformation. It coincides with the change in notary and is consistent with the observation that the last photos of Yvonne are from 1931.

Supporters of Mme Calment's authenticity have contested the earlier signature evidence [40, 41]. They point out that Yvonne's signature was quite different from the one used by Mme Calment. This is true, but signatures are stylised writing and Yvonne would change hers to try to match Jeanne's style. Unlike Jeanne, Yvonne did not use an underline tail from the final "t", and this was also the case for Mme Calment's version of the signature since 1933.

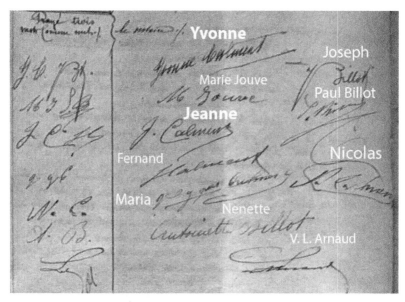

Signatures under Yvonne's marriage contract, 1926

Journalist Lauren Collins noted in an article written for the New Yorker magazine, that Jeanne signed documents in Arles in 1931 witnessed by the longstanding notary Victor Arnaud [34]. We have confirmed that the signatures from June and November that year were indeed in the style used by Jeanne. Collins considered this an important argument against the switch:

> *"In Zak's scenario, Yvonne had already started impersonating her mother in 1931. She would have shown up before Arnaud with her hair dyed white and a looping 'J' in her signature that wasn't quite right."* [34]

In fact, the Leysin pictures were from August and fell in the four-month interval between the signatures of June and November 1931. There is no reason to think she spent a longer period of time at the sanatorium there. Those foreigners who have lived in the commune of Leysin for more than 3 months should have been registered there, but the Calments were not found in the local archive.

Nor is there any reason to think that the identity switch took place before June 1932 when Arnaud retired. That was after the date of the last known signature written in Jeanne's style from February 1932. Collins believed that

> "Both Arnaud and David knew Jeanne too well to ask for identification,"

but Louis David had just recently moved to Arles and there is no evidence that he had ever met the family before 1933.

The signature evidence is therefore a perfect fit with the switch scenario and the inconsistencies claimed by others are not tenable.

Conclusion: Analysis of Jeanne Calment's signature provides strong evidence to support the identity switch hypothesis and indicates that the switch took place in 1932 or early 1933 about one year before the funeral for Yvonne in 1934.

IDENTITY CARD

I will say this body of work to validate the Jeanne Calment case as the all-time documented record holder is extremely impressive: we have solid proof of birth; we have solid proof of death; between the two, >40 documents and, even more than that, family-tree reconstitution, local area context, in-person interviews, and the like combine to make the Jeanne Calment case not just the oldest validated case but the best-validated case.

Robert Young [39]

Jeanne's ID card, 193? (face and back)

An identity card in the name of Jeanne Calment from the 1930s was preserved and reproduced in the biographies by Simonoff [69] and Cavalié [70]. The source has been attributed to Valerie Farine, but it is not known if it still exists.

Unfortunately, the scan of the reverse side was clipped so that the last numeral of the date is mostly not seen. We only know that it was issued on 11 January 193X.

The document was signed by Georges Valantin who was the central commissioner for Arles until August 11th, 1936, so X lies between 0 and 6 with the year 1931 excluded because the date was a Sunday. The small part of the digit visible fits best a 0, 3 or 6 although 2, 4 and 5 are not entirely ruled out.

Before the Second World War, such identity cards in the region of Arles were issued mainly to visitors from Italy who were obliged to register within three months of arrival in France. These documents can still be found at flea markets, but the style of Jeanne's ID is rare. Only two cards with such a design have been discovered, dated 1930 to 1932.

A card from Arles in 1934 has a different style so this makes 1934-1936 not plausible. The signature differs from those used by Jeanne until 1932 making 1930-1932 unlikely. The most probable year for the card is therefore 1933, but with some uncertainty.

François Robin-Champigneul who opposes the switch hypothesis believes that the correct year for the ID card is 1930 [40]. This is largely based on the VSD magazine that gave that date [88], but we know of no reason why the authors of the magazine article should have such information, and do not consider it a reliable source for that.

The date of 11th January 1933 would be just a month before Jeanne had to sign documents for the purchase of the villa in Paradou when we see changes in the signature. This raises the question as to whether the card was really obtained for Jeanne herself, or fraudulently by Yvonne to aid the change-over of identity.

Notice also that *Nom* and *Prenoms* fields: *"Calment"* and *"Jeanne ép(ouse) Calment"* loosely match how she signed documents in 1933. It is possible that the Identity Card was requested by the notary to verify her signature.

The picture on the card is genuinely Jeanne Calment. It corresponds in dress and hairstyle to another very similar one by the photographer Gustave Ouvière from the collection of Pierre Fassin. It must have been taken at the same studio session.

We don't know when Ouvière ended his career, but it seems likely that this photo was about ten years old in 1933, given the design of the matting that appeared in his work only since 1920, and the fact that we don't find his pictures taken after 1925.

The Arles Médiathèque dated it as 1900-1910, but our experience with other conserved photographs suggests that the dates provided by them are often not reliable.

The signature, on the other hand, corresponds very clearly to signatures used by Mme Calment from 1933 onward, and not to those of Jeanne from before 1932.

Furthermore, the card also had the name of *Paule Caumont* written on and was validated using a passport. This suggests that it was obtained by proxy without the bearer present. It also raises the question as to why Jeanne would need an ID card when she already had a passport. ID cards were not mandatory until a few years later, and if the passport was due to expire, she could have just renewed it.

These observations are consistent with the hypothesis that Yvonne procured this card at around the time of the switch to help her pose as her mother. She used a young photo of Jeanne where she looked like Yvonne. With this document she only had to change her hairstyle to be accepted as Jeanne in any official capacity.

Yvonne could have avoided being present when the card was verified so that the fraud was less likely to be discovered. In this case, she signed it in advance using a signature that she would replicate in the future. Even if Yvonne was present, she could fool the police officer because she was similar enough to the photo of Jeanne that she used.

We don't know why Yvonne needed this identity card, but it is highly likely that the new notary David required his new clients to bring identity documents. Perhaps the photo on Jeanne's passport was too different from Yvonne, so she decided to make an ID card with the photo which would not raise suspicions.

In a non-switch scenario, it is even more mysterious that Jeanne got an ID card that was unusual for locals in early 1930s, yet she did, so there had to be a reason. We think that Yvonne needed to get it in a hurry, because she apparently did not have time to accurately replicate her mother's signature from a sample.

The identity card supports the theory of the switch taking place about a year before the funeral for Yvonne. It also helps explain why it was hard for Yvonne to admit to the impersonation after Jeanne died. She would have to confess that she had committed signature fraud, a crime that would be very serious under French law.

Conclusion: If the identity card was really for use by Jeanne it raises a series of questions beyond the change of her signature. Why get a card several years before it became obligatory when she had a passport? Why use an old photo? Why not verify it in person?

If the card was obtained by Yvonne for her own fraudulent use these questions are naturally answered by her need to impersonate Jeanne before a new notary. The existence and nature of this card therefore supports the change of identity.

SWITCH PHOTO

It is true that the photo where she is with Yvonne, the one we published, has troubled many people, even scholars: the mother appears much more fit than the daughter.

M. Allard and J.-M. Robine [1]

The public evidence taken at face value seems to imply that Yvonne Calment died, while her mother Jeanne Calment went on to live for another 63 years.

In 1928 Joseph Billot temporarily resigned from the army. The reason given was that he was obliged to live near Arles to take care of his interests and the health of his wife. He was granted five years leave which was subsequently extended for another five years. During this time, he took part in occasional army drills but was otherwise free to be with his family. He reprised his full military duties in 1938 just before the start of World War Two.

In August 1931 Yvonne sent a photograph to her relatives

taken from the terrace of the Belvédère sanatorium in Leysin where patients were treated for tuberculosis. In January 1934 a funeral was held for Yvonne in Arles. The family reported that she had died of pleurisy, a common end stage of tuberculosis.

Those who support the authenticity of Mme Calment's longevity consider this to be good evidence that Yvonne remained ill while Jeanne was healthy [38, 40, 41], but additional findings suggest otherwise.

In late life Mme Calment said that she had never been ill *"Jamais, Jamais, Jamais"* she insisted. Because of her great age, some medical reports on her general state of health were prepared and are publicly available, though not easily obtained.

By chance an Envoyé Spécial documentary [32] showed a thesis written by Dr. Catherine Levraud [89]. A phrase about traces of pleural sequelae on the chest X-ray came into the frame.

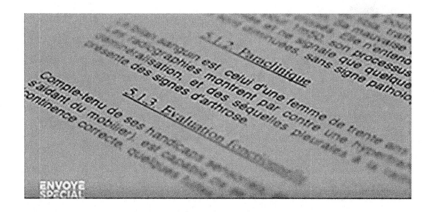

More details of the abnormalities are given by Garoyan

[90] p41. The medical reports also mention cataracts at age 20 that did not progress until late life. It would be difficult for an expert to give an opinion without access to the original X-ray images, but one possible cause of these symptoms could be a bout of tuberculosis in her past.

Assuming that this is correct the conclusion would be that regardless of which one died in 1934, both Jeanne and her daughter Yvonne had suffered from the infection, with one dying and the other surviving.

Madame Calment had told her validators that Yvonne became ill after giving birth to Freddy, that she was treated in a sanatorium in the *Haute Savoie*, and that she was not there for long [65] (25 and 26 Feb 1993 19:00). The photograph that Yvonne later sent from Leysin (this resort was never mentioned by Mme Calment) appears to show her in good health. She posed on a terrace as if on holiday and Robert Billot, nephew of Yvonne's husband who owns a copy of this photo, suggested that she was on vacation, but the location tells us otherwise.

The Belvédère was not only a sanatorium but also a hotel open to healthy visitors. There was a luxury restaurant under the terrace and a concert hall with good acoustics next to it. From June 1931 the famous pianist and wife of Doctor Miege, Jacqueline Blancard, played there frequently. However, there should have been a reason for Yvonne's decision to visit this hotel.

From audio recordings of interviews, we know that Mme Calment's doctor and validator Victor Lèbre had seen a copy of this photograph in early 1993 attributed as Jeanne [65] (25 Feb 1993 01:20 08:20; 25 and 26 Feb 1993 05:20; 10 Jun 1994 25:45). This is certainly incorrect.

Comparisons with other photos confirm that it was Yvonne, but Dr. Lèbre could not easily know that at the time.

[65] (25 and 26 Feb 1993 05:15)	Translation
VL: Je vous ai dit que j'avais vu une photo. J'ai vu une photo de vous lorsque que vous aviez à peu près 25 ans. MC: Ah oui? VL: Vous aviez une grande robe pantalon de plage et une ombrelle chinoise ou japonaise. MC: Hm. Oooh!!! Ne me rappelle pas ça. VL: Vous ne rappelez pas? MC: Non, no. VL: Vous posez avec une ombrelle Japonaise. MC: A c'est l'époque de jeunesse, à cette époque-là. VL: Vous vous rappelez de cette époque-là? MC: Naturellement, vaguement, c'est confus. VL: Vous ne rappelez pas	VL: I told you I saw a picture. I saw a picture of you when you were about 25 years old. MC: Oh yeah? VL: You had a big beach pants dress and a Chinese or Japanese umbrella (parasol). MC: Hm. Oooh!!! Don't remember that. VL: Don't recall? MC: No, no. VL: You're posing with a Japanese umbrella. MC: That's when I was young, that's when I was young. VL: Do you remember that time? MC: Naturally, vaguely, it's confusing. VL: Don't you remember that umbrella?

cette ombrelle? MC: Si! VL: Décrivez là moi un peu. MC: Ah, oh, ne me rappelle pas, ça je ne peux pas vous dire. VL: Sur la photo vous étiez éblouissante. MC: Étais jeune; quand on est jeune, on fait toujours de l'effet. VL: Vous étiez très séduisante. MC: Hm.	MC: Yes, I do! VL: Describe it to me. MC: Oh, oh, don't remember, I can't tell you that. VL: In the photo you were dazzling. MC: I was young; when you are young, you always make an impression. VL: You were very attractive. MC: Hm.

He asked about the photo several times complimenting her on her look. Mme Calment would not discuss the picture although she admitted at one point that she recognised the description.

(25 Feb 1993 01:40)	Translation
VL: Est-ce que vous vous rappelez ce moment-là? MC: No, Il y a trop de... Trop de tour malheureusement, il y a trop d'évènements depuis.	VL: Do you remember that time? MC: No, there's too many... Too many turns unfortunately, there's too many events since.

Why was she so evasive? Why would she not immediately tell him that it was in fact her daughter Yvonne?

We haven't found the journal from 1993, but in 1995, when Mme Calment reached the age of Moses and achieved the global fame, Yvonne from this image was reproduced as Jeanne by *Le Figaro* [91] and *The Times* [92].

Le Figaro, 1995   Leysin, 2020

Another well-known picture shows mother and daughter together. Yvonne's hairstyle matches perfectly the 1931 Leysin photo, so they could be taken on the same day, but now they are wearing formal dress while posing outside a ground-floor window. We refer to it as the *"switch photo"* since this is the last known picture of the Calments before the switch.

Yvonne   Jeanne

This iconic photo, first published by Michèle Gil in a local Arles newspaper and later reproduced in *Le Figaro* and in validators' books became the key to the Calment's secret of longevity. Even the validators had doubts over the picture:

Allard and Robine [1] p149	Translation
Il est vrai que la photo ou elle est avec Yvonne, celle que nous avons publiée, a troublé bien des gens, même savants: la mère y apparait bien plus en forme que la fille.	It is true that the photo where she is with Yvonne, the one we published, has troubled many people, even scholars: the mother appears much more fit than the daughter.

In recorded interviews Dr. Lèbre believed that it was Jeanne on the picture with umbrella. Since Yvonne's look is almost the same in the switch photo, the validators must have been confused about which of them is which here too.

To us the daughter seems healthier than the mother, but Robine and Allard assessed it the other way round because they misidentified them, as they later misidentified another picture of Yvonne as Jeanne in the Envoyé Spécial documentary [32].

On the switch photo, Jeanne has a wrapped present on the table in front of her and looks down on an arrangement of flowers which we believe to be carline thistle, a species of spiny stalkless flower that blooms in the alpine meadows in the late summer. A botanical census of Leysin from 1917 reported that Carlina Acaulis grew at the pastures near the chalet Palettaz which is seen behind Yvonne on her photo in Belvédère. They could certainly find more attractive flowers to give as a present but preferred carline thistle for its herbal properties: it was used as a remedy for chest infections including tuberculosis [93].

The switch photo provides us with a lot of useful details. Jeanne looks gaunt and appears to be darker than Yvonne as sunbathing was an essential part of treatment in Leysin. Not only the flowers, but also the curtains and the table on the picture match those seen on 1930s postcards from there.

In 2020 Nikolay Zak visited the former Belvédère sanatorium in Leysin (now a school of hotel management) and examined the windows overlooking the backyard, finding them to be similar in style and shape to the window in the picture.

Our opponents refused to accept that the switch photo was taken in Belvédère. They claimed that it was rather shot near Arles, either in the Mas de Rouiron or in the villa La Miquelette. However, the windows there are not compatible with the switch photo.

It was also argued that old postcards show that ground windows of Belvédère were protected with grids and therefore the photo could not be taken there.

We did see these grids on the west ground floor windows of the Belvédère in a picture from the early 1930s hanging in the nearby Hotel Mont Blanc. Perhaps the person talking through them to someone inside was familiar with Jeanne.

These bars were still there after Leysin switched from treating tuberculosis to a touristic resort and Belvédère became the Club Med Hotel. Later they were removed, leaving openings in the windowsills.

Thanks to the rare 1948 aerial photo by Werner Friedli which shows the central part of the garden, we can see two united windows which, together with the door, are located exactly in the center of the main part of the building. It seems likely that these windows led to the guarded hall, and the bars there could be temporarily removed after the renovation of the building prior to the reopening of the sanatorium in the end of 1930.

Being initially in the center of the building, this pair of windows could have replaced a former entrance. Curiously, a paved road leads directly to them and not to the current door on the right. It was therefore an appropriate place for a photo session in formal attire for patients at the Belvédère.

However, the possibility that this window might have had grilles in 1931, and the lack of reflections in the switch photo, led us to investigate further: could it have been taken on a higher terrace?

The lack of shade on either side of Yvonne's nose suggests that she is roughly facing the sun, but to get a better idea of the circumstances we made a model using the plasticine figures created by Agata Zak.

Modelling the switch photo (figures by Agata Zak)

The model shows that for the shadow pattern seen in the switch photo, the light should be coming from ~33 degrees to the right of Jeanne's position, and the sun's elevation should be ~26 degrees above the horizon, with a possible variation of about 5 degrees.

Yvonne's appearance is very close to the photo with the parasol, which is dated August, the time of year when the carline thistle blooms, so we believe that the switch photo was also taken in August. The ground floor terrace is therefore inconsistent with the position of the sun, which would be too high on the south side for the shadow pattern in the photograph.

On the other hand, this pattern is plausible for 8:30 in the morning on the higher terrace of the Belvédère, facing northeast to east. The shadows in the picture of Yvonne with the parasol suggest that it was taken an hour later.

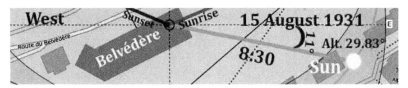

Position of the sun on the terrace based on suncalc.org

We have been searching for the possible locations for the switch photo for years and have had numerous discussions with François Robin-Champigneul and others. Most of the windows in Leysin that we checked were not suitable for the photo, but the window in front of Yvonne's position at the corner of the terrace seems to be a good match.

On the north side of the building, windows of the same size have survived, and they appear to match the switch photo. The height of the windowsill is also consistent, and we even found footage of doctors looking at x-rays on a neighbouring window in the 1935 film about Leysin.

The windows in Belvédère usually appear with some small horizontal bars supporting the glass from the inside, but these bars were easy to move and it is possible that they were not there in August 1931. Overall, there is a good chance that the switch photo was taken at almost the same place and time as the photo of Yvonne alone.

Unfortunately, we can't reconstruct the photos of Calments on the terrace because it was built over in the late 1960s to add more rooms to the hotel.

Switch photo was probably taken in front of Yvonne's position at the terrace of Belvedere

It could be that on a sunny morning in August 1931 they took a picture of Jeanne receiving gifts from Yvonne on the terrace of the Belvédère. Yvonne was then photographed alone with a view that would not reveal her location, and the postcards with this photo were sent to her friends and family. Sixty-six years later, one of them died in Arles as the oldest human ever.

In 1934, the famous avant-garde artist Alexander de Salzmann died at Belvedere. The atmosphere of the sanatorium was described by Solange Batsell, who was treated there in 1946, at the beginning of the antibiotic era:

> *"Even before I could finish my thesis, I was shipped off to a TB sanitarium in Switzerland. I languished*

142

in that hospital for an endless year. It was in Leysin and was called 'Le Belvédère'. The miracle cure for tuberculosis in those days was lots of fresh air. No moderate exercise, not any exercise.

They simply bundled you up in a chaise longue and abandoned you to a terrace, all the live-long day to 'rest'. We would dress for dinner - ladies in long dresses, gentlemen in black tie. Every night! A musical ensemble played for us all through dinner.

Patients included Russians, Germans, a sprinkling of French, Swiss, English and many Indians and Pakistanis. And some of these patients had been there for years. A few had their own entourage, friends, servants, musicians, hairdressers, etc. It was all pretty grand. One prized patient was Sir Stafford Cripps, Great Britain's Chancellor of the Exchequer.

A highlight of each day was when the huge black chukka birds came flying around to battle each other for breakfast crumbs. To me, they looked like circling vultures casing the joint to see who was going to expire next. And indeed, people died. We would notice an empty seat in the dining room, the grim signal that another companion was gone and there would be a tightening of the ranks. But my luck held as it has so often.

While I was there, they discovered the first wonder drug to fight tuberculosis, PAS. I was one of the first patients to be given large doses of it. The effects were unbelievably fast." [94]

The switch photo is interesting to compare with a picture from a Paris Match report [95] showing Jeanne Calment at her home a few years earlier. Robert Billot has testified confidently that the woman on the photo absolutely does not appear to him to be the lady he knew only a decade later. However, the authenticity of the picture as Jeanne Calment is not in doubt, her face matches that of an earlier undisputed photo of Jeanne.

The comparison shows that in Leysin Jeanne had lost

a considerable amount of weight, unlike her daughter. Weight loss, known as cachexia, is a hallmark of pulmonary tuberculosis and is associated with poor prognosis. It is hard to avoid the conclusion that it was Jeanne who was ill and at the Belvédère sanatorium for treatment.

One final picture shows a group of ladies from *"l'Escolo Mistralenco"* on a carnival float, dated July 1931. On the left at the front Yvonne in her distinguishing Charles X bow tie headdress can once again be identified, with some uncertainty.

It seems unlikely that Yvonne would be participating in this activity if she needed treatment for tuberculosis in Leysin the following month. She had certainly been ill earlier, but by 1931 it was Jeanne's health that was the cause for concern.

To conclude, the medical assessments of Mme Calment indicate that she probably had an earlier episode of tuberculosis and therefore both Yvonne and Jeanne had the disease in the period 1927 to 1934. In 1931 when they were photographed in Leysin it was most likely Jeanne who was ill, while Yvonne had already recovered.

DOCTOR MAURICE GILBERT

Sanatorium BELVÉDÈRE

OUVERTURE LE 15 NOVEMBRE 1930

Direction médicale : **M. le Dr Maurice GILBERT.**

Prix de Pension, soins médicaux compris, à partir de 13 fr. 50 par jour.

Pour visiter et réserver les chambres, ainsi que pour tous renseignements administratifs s'adresser à M. E. PLATEL, gérant du ,, Belvédère ''.

W e found Jeanne and Fernand Calment listed in the August 1911 issue of the Montreux Journal of Foreigners, staying at the Grand

Hotel Suisse. However, our search for 1931 was in vain because, unlike the neighbouring resorts, Leysin hadn't provided the Journal with its list of visitors for reasons of confidentiality.

Instead, the Société Climatérique de Leysin published multiple advertisements offering the treatment of pulmonary tuberculosis in their sanatoriums, taking the advantage of the altitude, air, and sun. Among the head doctors mentioned on the adverts we found Dr. Maurice Gilbert (1896-1980).

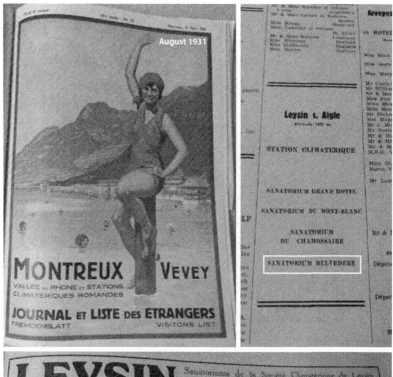

Before taking his position in the renovated Belvédère in 1930, Dr. Gilbert worked with Dr. René Burnard in sanatorium Populaire in Leysin and then in the Fuad I sanatorium in Egypt, invited by the king.

As the son of the famous painter Eugène Burnard who illustrated Mistral's Mireille, René maintained a correspondence with Madame Mistral until the 1940s. Mme Calment said that Fernand was a friend of the poet, so they could have found out about Dr. Gilbert through Dr. Burnard.

A trip near Leysin, 1925 (collection of Philippe Chappuis)

In 1932 Dr. Gilbert married Paulette Kellner, his patient in Leysin who suffered from tuberculosis, and they had two children. One of them, Luc-Régis Gilbert, became a distinguished architect.

We first published the conclusion that both Jeanne and Yvonne had contracted tuberculosis in our Bayesian analysis paper [48]. Since then, we have been searching for their names in archives related to patients or visitors to Leysin, but nothing has turned up so far.

Nevertheless, we found convincing evidence to support our case, the most important of which was the testimony of Luc-Régis Gilbert whom we were able to contact by e-mail, telephone and video call.

Dr. Maurice Gilbert died in 1980, before Mme Calment became famous for her longevity, but his son recalled for us that at some time in 1970s his father had spoken to his children about his surprise to discover that Jeanne Calment from Arles was still alive.

Jeanne had been treated by Dr. Gilbert in Leysin, and he was delighted that his former patient who was much older than himself had survived that long. His son recalled him joking:

"I've treated this person and I'll probably die before her because I have treated her well."

From this description we can be sure that he was talking of Jeanne and not of Yvonne who was younger than him. Luc-Régis told us that his father had never mentioned Jeanne Calment's daughter.

We are not aware of how Dr. Gilbert learnt of Jeanne's long survival, but we know that he had a vacation residence in Gordes since 1970 and could have visited Arles that was not far away. He might have recognised the Calment name still displayed above their former shop where it remains even today, and could easily have found out that Mme Calment was still there from a conversation with locals.

It is equally possible that, as suggested by his son, she could appear in the local news, perhaps on the occasion of her 100th birthday when she visited the mayor of Arles and astonished him with her youthful appearance. She was sufficiently well-known at that time to be interviewed by a local historian Garagnon in 1977.

However he made the discovery, Dr. Gilbert found it remarkable enough to mention to his children.

Luc-Régis also mentioned that his father advised patients to spend less time in a sanatorium. He was in favour of outpatient treatment in the community, so that the sick person would spend more time with his family. We know that the Calments followed his advice and bought the villa in Paradou for this purpose.

We thank Luc-Régis for his time and kindness to share this very important testimony. The video recording of our Zoom meeting on December 14, 2022 is available online at https://www.youtube.com/watch?v=8TNrXdagQRM. Here is the transcript:

Ilya: *Hello, my name is Ilya and I help Nikolay Zak and Philip Gibbs in the investigation of Jeanne Calment's longevity. Today, December 14, 2022, we will conduct an interview with the architect Luc-Régis Gilbert, son of Dr. Maurice Gilbert who died in 1980 and who, in the 1930s, would have treated Jeanne Calment for tuberculosis at the Belvedere Sanatorium of Leysin.*

Let me introduce Mr. Gilbert and thank him again for agreeing to this interview. We contacted Mr. Gilbert for the first time in 2020 after visiting Leysin and discovering that his father was the head doctor of the Belvedere. Since then, we have communicated several times by email and phone, and Mr. Gilbert's testimony was included in the first volume of the book "Jeanne Calment, the secret of longevity unravelled."

We will ask Mr. Gilbert a few questions to confirm the information that has already been published previously, so hello Mr. Gilbert.

Mr. Gilbert: *Hello.*

Ilya: *You said that at one point, your father told you about Jeanne Calment, who was his patient at the Belvedere, still alive despite her advanced age. If I understand correctly, it was in the 1960s or 1970s, when she was younger than 105 because your father died in 1980, when Jeanne Calment was 105.*

Mr. Gilbert: *Yes, what you are saying is true. It was rather sudden. I don't know why, but it was more like a joke, because my father was at that time in Leysin, he was a young doctor, and he remembered this person who was mentioned on the radio or in the press as being very old. And then he would laugh and say,*

"I treated this person and I'm probably going to die before her because I treated her well."

It was a joke.

Nikolay: *Which year was that? 1970s?*

Mr. Gilbert: *I no longer have a very specific memory, I think it was in our house in Gordes, that we had discussed this, but I do not remember either* *the occasion or the precise reason, you know, it is very old already. It has been almost 50 years and so I do not know exactly. In any case, I remember very well that my father started laughing and said, "this person was amazing". So, he got to know her well. In Leysin, in Leysin, indeed my father was a doctor who specialized in phthisiology, the subject of tuberculosis, and he was very obviously motivated by the fact of the arrival of antibiotics.*

And it was there that he met his wife who had come from Paris to be treated in Leysin also for the reason of the disease, tuberculosis.

Nikolay: *Perhaps they were friends with Jeanne Calment, and that's why he remembered her?*

Mr. Gilbert: *He remembered her because he had treated her. You know, at the time, the doctors were courteous and very attached to their patients, they talked, and especially in Leysin where there was a kind of family isolation, and that is the reason why my father denied the use of a sanatorium by recommending that all patients stay with their families rather than leave their families and go to a sanatorium to isolate themselves.*

You know that the book by Thomas Mann tells this well, about this period when people isolated themselves completely and when they came down, it was to find an abandonment of the family. And so, my father thought it was much better to treat on an outpatient basis. That is, in the town where the patient lived. And as antibiotics arrived, he was able to treat not only many people in Switzerland, but he also did a lot to save lives in France, despite the German occupation that raged from 39 to 45.

Ilya: *Correct me if I've got it wrong, in the 1970s, presumably, your father would have heard about Madame Calment on the radio or elsewhere? And it is on this occasion...*

Mr. Gilbert: *In the press. On the radio or in the press.*

Ilya: *In the press, that's it, and that's when he told you about her.*

Mr. Gilbert: *Yes, that is correct. So, the occasion I don't know, but it was quite as I tell you. Perhaps it was simply through the radio, and he was startled by the fact that he had known this person once. Long before, so I had already, in the 1970s... since I was born in '37, you see that it was in '37, it was the time when he was still in Leysin.*

Ilya: *When he told you about Madame Calment, did he have any other interesting memories to share? Did he talk about her family, or her daughter?*

Mr. Gilbert: *No, her daughter's story, I understood it afterwards, we did not talk much about her* *daughter at that time. In the period of the 70s, at least for my own part, and my father hadn't made any reference to her daughter. And then it was understood that her daughter had some difficulties with the truth. Whether this is true what she said about her mother because she wanted to profit from her mother's inheritance, I think. There was certainly something, but I can't tell you about it because I will only tell you nonsense or inaccuracies.*

Nikolay: *Is it possible that he confused the mother and the daughter? Is it possible that he treated the daughter and not the mother?*

Mr. Gilbert: *No, I think it was the mother whom he treated because he was aware of how old she was, which was quite exceptional. And that was why he started laughing when he talked about that. And I just told you that he said she would die after him, when he was already of advanced age in 1970s, I don't know exactly how old he was.*

Nikolay: *He never told you anything about her daughter? Did you know that she had a daughter?*

Mr. Gilbert: *No, I did not hear from him at all about that. I never heard from him about her daughter. Unfortunately.*

Nikolay: *And this story of Jeanne Calment, your father shared it only with you, or also with your* *family, your sister, maybe?*

Mr. Gilbert: *My sister was certainly there when he spoke to us about Jeanne Calment. But my sister passed away, so you can't ask her for anything, and I'm the one who has all these records because we were just two siblings, there were no other siblings. In other words, in my whole family, I am the oldest, the most motivated to collect all the archives and memories. You did well to find me. I lost a first cousin 3 years ago. He was very competent in the memories of my Swiss family, including the family of my father, but all this will not give you anything more about Madame Calment.*

Nikolay: *Was that the only time, perhaps in 1970s, when he told you about Jeanne Calment, but you still remember it?*

Mr. Gilbert: *Well, maybe he told us about her afterwards, you know, it was verbal, and I don't remember. But she was someone that we had, I would say, adopted into our memory. Because when we talked about her, it brought back the memories. You know, maybe we were joking because in the meantime Madame Calment was slowly getting older and then she became so old. And that surprised everybody. She was becoming a very special person in the whole world.*

It's a part of my life when I was an architect, an urban planner, and a teacher, so I was in the middle of my professional practice in the 1970s. And it makes me very happy to have these memories, but I am sorry not to be able to give you much more, and it is thanks to you that I relive this period in the history of Madame Calment and my father. It is probably through his story that we understood who this person was. He had no reason to tell us about her except that she was very old. He had heard when they talked about her on the radio.

Nikolay: *Perhaps, he visited Arles and he saw the Calment store with big letters "Calment", and someone told him that she was still alive, maybe like this?*

Mr. Gilbert: *Well, I don't know... We had a house in Gordes, in the south of France. And it could be that he went to Arles, but I do not remember that he was aware of the store you are talking about. The house in Gordes we have had since 1970, but I don't remember exactly. Perhaps he spoke about Jeanne Calment when we were still living in Geneve, but I don't have any precise memories of that. But this is not impossible.*

Nikolay: *She was 100 years old in 1975. That was perhaps that moment?*

Mr. Gilbert: *Yes. But I repeat that my father didn't talk about his patients due to the professional secret. So, there would be no reason why he would talk to us about her, neither my sister, nor myself,* *at the time when we were... Since 1956 my sister went to live in Paris, and I went to Oxford for one year. So, since 1956 we were not living together with my father. My father remained in Geneve, and we moved to Paris for our studies and then for our professional career. My sister was three years older than me.*

Nikolay: *If he knew she was alive, perhaps he wanted to talk to her?*

Mr. Gilbert: *I don't know about that. And she probably didn't stay in Leysin for a long time. I don't know how many years if it's even years. She probably came there for treatment, for a year or I don't know how long. But she didn't stay there, she left, I guess, after the first treatment. And, once again, my father was not in a friendly relationship with her, as he wasn't with the other patients. He had no reason to have a particular friendship with Jeanne Calment. In any case, I would certainly have known if he would have spoken of her as his friend, but that was not the case.*

Conclusion: The testimony from the family of Dr. Gilbert confirms that Jeanne was treated for tuberculosis in Leysin in 1931. If Yvonne had tuberculosis in 1928 or earlier, then she had most likely recovered. We believe that evidence suggesting that both Yvonne and Jeanne were ill before 1932 is sufficiently strong that this can be accepted for both the base and the switch scenarios.

If Yvonne had relapsed after 1931, they would probably have also taken her to Dr. Gilbert for treatment. This is not consistent with memories of his son who didn't know anything about Jeanne's daughter.

Mme Calment had never mentioned Belvédère and said that Yvonne received a short treatment in *Haute Savoie* after the birth of Freddy. This favours the scenario where Jeanne and not Yvonne died from tuberculosis in 1934.

Mme Calment was reluctant to give any clues related to Leysin to her relatives, friends and validators who were not aware of her real identity.

In the following volume we will continue to review the details of the extraordinary *life* of Mme Calment and produce the Bayesian table for all the available evidence according to the method.

THANKS

This report would not have been complete without the numerous historical discoveries of Patricia Laurette Hussenet Couturier. We are also grateful to Christian Grant, Ilya Krouglikov, Marguerite Raspail, Georges E. Melki and Cyril Depoudent for their help and finds, Bernadette Murphy and Galina Shagieva for very thorough review and helpful suggestions and to Sergey Galkin, Jean-Charles Simon, Gerard Lelieveld, and many others for their support.

We also thank our opponent François Robin-Champigneul for interesting findings, respectful discussion, and fruitful debates, and all those who shared their discoveries and raised counterarguments against the switch scenario for helping us to refine it.

Last but not least, we would like to thank Mme Calment, her validators, relatives, and countrymen for providing the unique material for analysis. We thank them wholeheartedly for their inestimable contributions to this work.

BIBLIOGRAPHY

[1]   M. Allard and J.-M. Robine, Les centenaires francias. Etude de la fondation IPSEN, Paris: Serdi, 2001.

[2]   J. Oeppen and J. W. Vaupel, "Broken Limits to Life expectancy," *Science's Compass, Policy forum on Demography,* vol. 296, 10 May 2002.

[3]   E. Dolgin, "There's no limit to longevity, says study that revives human lifespan debate," Nature, June 2018. [Online]. Available: https://www.nature.com/articles/d41586-018-05582-3.

[4]   J.-M. Robine and M. Allard, "The Oldest Human," *Science,* vol. 279, no. 5358, p. 1831, March 1998.

[5]   H. Maier, B. Jeune and J. W. Vaupel, Exceptional Lifespans, Springer, 2021.

[6]   D. Stipp, "Hell No, We Won't Go! Surprising demographic trends raise a tough question: Will the elderly live so long that society can't cope?," *CNN Money, Fortune Magazine,* 19 July 1999.

[7]   "More of Us on Track to Reach Age 100: Genes,

Habits, Baboons Examined for Longevity Clues," Population Reference Bureau, June 2011. [Online]. Available: https://www.prb.org/resources/more-of-us-on-track-to-reach-age-100-genes-habits-baboons-examined-for-longevity-clues/.

[8]   "AXA Global forum for Longevity," 2011.

[9]   B. Bouskila, "Étude de la longévité du portefeuille vie individuelle d'AXA France. Gestion des risques.," 2013.

[10]   A. de Vos, "Longevity improvements will continue, says demographics expert," September 2018. [Online]. Available: https://www.ipe.com/longevity-improvements-will-continue-says-demographics-expert/10026807.article.

[11]   P. Gibbs and N. Zak, "A Review of Longevity Validations to 2020," April 2021. [Online]. Available: https://www.researchgate.net/publication/350735049_A_Review_of_Longevity_Validations_to_2020.

[12]   S. J. Olshansky and B. A. Carnes, "Inconvenient Truths About Human Longevity," *J Gerontol A Biol Sci Med Sci*, vol. 74, no. Suppl_1, pp. S7-S12, Nov 2019.

[13]   "Twenty million adults could be in line for 'state pension age reprieve' as life expectancy improvements 'collapse' even before the

Pandemic," LCP, December 2021. [Online].
Available: https://www.lcp.uk.com/media-centre/2021/12/twenty-million-adults-could-be-in-line-for-state-pension-age-reprieve-as-life-expectancy-improvements-collapse-even-before-the-pandemic/.

[14] "Life expectancy gap between rich and poor widens," BBC, February 2018. [Online]. Available: https://www.bbc.co.uk/news/health-43058394.

[15] R. Karma, "The Gross Inequality of Death in America," The New Republic, May 2019. [Online]. Available: https://newrepublic.com/article/153870/inequality-death-america-life-expectancy-gap.

[16] P. Dizikes, "New study shows rich, poor have huge mortality gap in U.S.," MIT News, April 2016. [Online]. Available: https://news.mit.edu/2016/study-rich-poor-huge-mortality-gap-us-0411.

[17] W. Audureau, "Qu'est-ce que l'« espérance de vie en bonne santé », indicateur récurrent des débats sur l'âge de départ à la retraite ?," Le Monde, 15 April 2022. [Online]. Available: https://www.lemonde.fr/les-decodeurs/article/2022/04/15/qu-est-ce-que-l-esperance-de-vie-en-bonne-sante-indicateur-recurrent-des-debats-sur-l-age-de-depart-a-la-retraite_6122315_4355770.html.

[18] N. Brouard, "Calculs sur la longevity,"
Institut National d'Etudes Démographiques,
June 1995. [Online]. Available: https://
web.archive.org/web/20010221055208/http://
www.centenaire.com/Science/Valid.htm.

[19] J.-M. Robine, "Jeanne Calment and the supercentenarians," *Gérontologie et société*, vol. 43, no.
166, pp. 11-23, September 2021.

[20] E. Milova, "Valery Novoselov: Investigating
Jeanne Calment's Longevity Record," Lifespan.io,
December 2018. [Online]. Available: https://
www.lifespan.io/news/valery-novoselov-
investigating-jeanne-calments-longevity-
record/.

[21] V. Novoselov, "The Consequences of The
Professional Geriatric Evaluation of The Oldest
Human," *Gerontology & Geriatrics Studies*, vol. 4,
no. 4, March 2019.

[22] N. Zak, "Нестарение или пожизненная рента,"
*Proceedings of the Gerontology Section of the
Moscow Society of Naturalists* , October 2018.

[23] N. Zak, "Jeanne Calment: the secret of longevity,"
19 Dec 2018. [Online]. Available: https://
www.researchgate.net/
publication/329773795_Jeanne_Calment_the_se
cret_of_longevity.

[24]   N. Zak, "Evidence That Jeanne Calment Died in 1934—Not 1997," *Rejuvenation Research,* vol. 22, no. 1, February 2019.

[25]   N. Zak, 2018. [Online]. Available: https://onedrive.live.com/?authkey=%21AGi8GSxD8Nv8hKY&cid=41B8120C989594F7&id=41B8120C989594F7%21181637&parId=root&o=OneUp.

[26]   R. Baheux, "Jeanne Calment, une imposture ? Le scientifique qui a validé son record s'insurge," L Parisien, December 2018. [Online]. Available: https://www.leparisien.fr/societe/jeanne-calment-une-imposture-le-scientifique-qui-a-valide-son-record-s-insurge-30-12-2018-7978578.php.

[27]   G. Gobet, "Des chercheurs russes remettent en question l'âge de la mort de Jeanne Calment," Le Monde, January 2019. [Online]. Available: https://www.lemonde.fr/societe/article/2019/01/01/jeanne-calment-etait-elle-vraiment-la-doyenne-de-l-humanite_5404134_3224.html.

[28]   M. Rubetti, "Des Russes remettent en cause l'âge de Jeanne Calment, doyenne de l'humanité," Le Figaro, January 2019. [Online]. Available: https://www.lefigaro.fr/actualite-france/2019/01/01/01016-20190101ARTFIG00127-des-russes-remettent-en-cause-l-age-de-

jeanne-calment-doyenne-de-l-humanite.php.

[29]   E. Rosenberg, "The world's oldest person record stood for decades. Then came a Russian conspiracy theory," Washington Post, January 2019. [Online]. Available: https://www.washingtonpost.com/world/2019/01/12/how-madame-calment-worlds-oldest-person-became-fuel-russian-conspiracy-theory/.

[30]   C. L. Pomellec, "L'affaire Jeanne Calment," Je t'aime etc, March 2019. [Online]. Available: https://www.youtube.com/watch?v=g9GyVvqQ1Vc.

[31]   "Le mystère Jeanne Calment," C l'hebdo, March 2019. [Online]. Available: https://www.youtube.com/watch?v=1-NTjLN2okg.

[32]   O. Sibille, M. Dreujou and H. Horoks, "L'énigme Jeanne Calment," Envoyé Spécial, France 2, March 2019. [Online]. Available: https://actu.orange.fr/societe/videos/replay-jeanne-calment-a-t-elle-vraiment-vecu-jusqu-a-122-ans-regardez-l-enquete-d-envoye-special-sur-la-doyenne-de-l-humanite-CNT000001dX8wO.html.

[33]   P. Hoad, "'People are caught up in magical thinking': was the oldest woman in the world a fraud?," The Guardian, November 2019. [Online]. Available: https://www.theguardian.com/science/2019/nov/30/oldest-woman-in-the-world-magical-thinking.

[34] L. Collins, "Was Jeanne Calment the Oldest Person Who Ever Lived—or a Fraud?," New Yorker, February 2020. [Online]. Available: https://www.newyorker.com/ magazine/2020/02/17/was-jeanne-calment-the-oldest-person-who-ever-lived-or-a-fraud.

[35] "Clarifications by Inserm following the fraud allegations surrounding the age of Jeanne Calment," INSERM, January 2019. [Online]. Available: https://presse.inserm.fr/en/mise-au-point-de-linserm-suite-aux-allegations-de-fraudes-relatives-a-lage-de-jeanne-calment/33420/.

[36] É. L. Bourg, "Jeanne Calment's daughter usurped her mother's identity - An amateur work or scientific research ?," *Med Sci,* vol. 35, no. 4, p. 375–380, April 2019.

[37] E. L. Bourg, ""Jeanne Calment's daughter has usurped her mother's identity": an amateur work or scientific research?," English translation, 2019. [Online]. Available: https://www.medecinesciences.org/en/articles/medsci/olm/2019/05/msc190028/msc190028-olm.pdf.

[38] J.-M. Robine, M. Allard, F. R. Herrmann and B. Jeune, "The Real Facts Supporting Jeanne Calment as the Oldest Ever Human," *The Journals of Gerontology: Series A,* vol. 74, p. S13–S20, 2019.

[39]   R. Young, "If Jeanne Calment Were 122, That
         Is All the More Reason for Biosampling,"
         Rejuvenation Research, vol. 23, no. 1, February
         2020.

[40]   F. Robin-Champigneul, "Jeanne Calment's Unique
         122-Year Life Span: Facts and Factors; Longevity
         History in Her Genealogical Tree," *Rejuvenation
         Research,* vol. 23, no. 1, February 2020.

[41]   M. Perny-Villeneuve, "Counter-Investigation
         about Jeanne Calment's Longevity," posted as
         comment to Plos Biology paper by Gavrilovs,
         February 2019. [Online]. Available: https://
         journals.plos.org/plosbiology/article/comment?
         id=10.1371/annotation/8eb167cb-db79-42b7-
         a293-7958ce458de1.

[42]   "Affaire Jeanne Calment : le dénouement," C
         l'hebdo, September 2020. [Online]. Available:
         https://www.youtube.com/watch?v=-
         Jv3qlWQmAg.

[43]   "Nouvelles révélations sur l'âge de Jeanne
         Calment," Le Figaro, September 2019. [Online].
         Available: https://sante.lefigaro.fr/article/
         nouvelles-revelations-sur-l-age-de-jeanne-
         calment/.

[44]   N. Herzberg, "Ni complot ni fraude : Jeanne
         Calment était bien Jeanne Calment," Le Monde,
         September 2020. [Online]. Available: https://

www.lemonde.fr/sciences/article/2019/09/16/
jeanne-calment-l-hypothese-d-une-fraude-
familiale-demontee_5510841_1650684.html.

[45]   R. Baheux, "Affaire Jeanne Calment : de
nouveaux arguments pour balayer la
théorie russe," September 2019. [Online].
Available: https://www.leparisien.fr/societe/
affaire-jeanne-calment-des-nouveaux-
arguments-pour-balayer-la-theorie-
russe-16-09-2019-8152719.php.

[46]   BBC, "France insists world's 'oldest woman'
was not fake," [Online]. Available: https://
www.bbc.co.uk/news/world-europe-49746060.

[47]   J.-C. Laurence, "Débat international sur l'identité
de la doyenne de l'humanité," La Press, Sep 2019.
[Online]. Available: https://www.lapresse.ca/
international/europe/2019-09-21/debat-
international-sur-l-identite-de-la-doyenne-de-l-
humanite.

[48]   N. Zak and P. Gibbs, "A Bayesian Assessment of
the Longevity of Jeanne Calment," *Rejuvenation
Research*, vol. 23, no. 1, February 2020.

[49]   C. Vial, "Affaire Jeanne Calment : le procureur
de Tarascon n'ouvrira pas de procédure
de rectification d'état civil," La Provence,
September 2019. [Online]. Available: https://
www.laprovence.com/article/edition-
arles/5678938/le-parquet-ne-donnera-pas-de-

suites-judiciaires.html.

[50] R. Baheux, "Jeanne Calment : la justice refuse de changer l'âge de la doyenne de l'humanité," Le Parisien, September 2019. [Online]. Available: https://www.leparisien.fr/societe/jeanne-calment-la-justice-refuse-de-changer-l-age-de-la-doyenne-de-l-humanite-18-09-2019-8154834.php.

[51] P. Collinson and M. Brignall, "Pension firms profit from slowdown in life expectancy growth," The Guardian, August 2018. [Online]. Available: https://www.theguardian.com/money/2018/aug/09/billion-pound-bonanza-for-life-insurers-over-slowdown-in-life-expectancy-pension.

[52] R. Baheux, "Pourquoi la science se déchire sur l'affaire Jeanne Calment," Le Parisien, January 2019. [Online]. Available: https://www.leparisien.fr/societe/pourquoi-la-science-se-dechire-sur-l-affaire-jeanne-calment-24-01-2019-7996305.php.

[53] J.-C. Lamy, Le Mystere de la chambre Jeanne Calment, Fayard, 2013.

[54] M. Maria Cuellar, L. A. and J. Mauro, "A probabilistic formalization of contextual bias in forensic analysis: Evidence that examiner bias leads to systemic bias in the criminal justice system," 2021.

[55]   S. Jackman, Bayesian Analysis for the Social
        Sciences, Wiley Series in Probability and
        Statistics, 2009.

[56]   S. E. Fienberg, "When Did Bayesian Inference
        Become," *Bayesian Analysis*, vol. 1, no. 1, pp. 1-40,
        2006.

[57]   S. B. McGrayne, The Theory That Would Not
        Die: How Bayes' Rule Cracked The Enigma Code,
        Hunted Down Russian Submarines, & Emerged
        Triumphant from Two Centuries of Controversy.,
        New Haven: Yale University Press, 2011.

[58]   E. Lennert and C. Bridge, "Review: Forensic
        Statistics 101: The Bayesian Approach and
        Common Fallacies," 2017.

[59]   T. Nugent, The grand tour, or a journey through
        the Netherlands, Germany, Italy and France, vol.
        4, 1756.

[60]   "Van Gogh Museum, Letters," [Online]. Available:
        http://vangoghletters.org/vg/.

[61]   C. Mathieu, M. Dunham and C. Porlier, "Quand
        Jeanne Calment confiait ses souvenirs à Paris
        Match," 2019. [Online]. Available: https://
        www.parismatch.com/Actu/Societe/Ete-88-
        Jeanne-Calment-la-mamie-du-monde-1566969.

[62]   J.-P. Poly, La Provence et la societe feodale, Paris,

1976.

[63]   F. Mistral, Lou Tresor dóu Felibrige.

[64]   R.-A. Michel, "Une accusation de meurtre rituel contre les Juifs d'Uzès en 1297," *Bibliothèque de l'École des chartes,* vol. 75, pp. 59-66, 1914.

[65]   V. Lèbre, M. Allard, J. Calment and J.-M. Robine, "Fonds audio Jeanne Calment," Inserm, January 2022. [Online]. Available: https://www.ipubli.inserm.fr/handle/10608/12340.

[66]   Revue du Midi, vol. 21, 1897.

[67]   C. B. Boyer, "Genealogy of the Calment family," *Gérontologie et société,* vol. 43, no. 166, pp. 109-119, September 2021.

[68]   E. Fassin, Bulletin archéologique d'Arles. Archeologic Society of Arles, 1889-1891.

[69]   G. Simonoff, Jeanne Calment: La passion de vivre, Du Rocher, 1998.

[70]   F. Cavalié, Jeanne Calment: Loubliée de Dieu, Paris: TF1, 1995.

[71]   "The Antituberculosis Crusade in France," *The Journal of the American Medical Association,* vol. 87, no. 17, pp. 1405-1406, October 1926.

[72]   M. Herzberg, I. Mandraud and F. Aubenas, "Jeanne

Calment, L'Arlésienne," *Le Monde,* 15 Feb 2019.

[73]   M. Allard, V. Lebre and J.-M. Robine, Jeanne
       Calment from Van Gogh's time to ours, 122
       extraordinary years, New York: W. H. Freeman,
       1998.

[74]   M. Allard, V. Lebre and J.-M. Robine, Les 120 ans
       de Jeanne Calment, Doyenne de l'humanity, Paris:
       le cherche midi, 1994.

[75]   D. Rouard, "Jeanne Calment, cent treize ans,
       doyenne des Français," *Le Monde,* 9 Dec 1988.

[76]   C. Porlier, "la Mammy du Monde," *Paris Match,* no.
       2040, pp. 88-93, July 1988.

[77]   L. D. Cock and H. Michiels, Onze goede vriendin,
       Jeanne Calment, La doyenne de l'humanity,
       www.koleltiva.be, 2020.

[78]   M. Enault, "Jeanne Calment : le témoignage
       de sa plus proche parente," Le Journal du
       Dimanche, January 2019. [Online]. Available:
       https://www.lejdd.fr/Societe/jeanne-
       calment-le-temoignage-de-sa-plus-proche-
       parente-3845306.

[79]   C. Le Pomellec, "Jeanne Calment : notre contre-
       enquête," Paris Match, March 2019. [Online].
       Available: https://www.parismatch.com/
       Actu/Societe/Jeanne-Calment-notre-contre-
       enquete-1601145.

[80] "The oldest person in the world still full of wit," *Gisborne Gerald*, 22 Feb 1995.

[81] "121-year-old french woman revels in newfound celebrity," *Desert News, London Observer Service*, 21 Feb 1996.

[82] T. Kirkwood, Time of Our Lives: The Science of Human Aging, Oxford University Press, 1999.

[83] H. Roselmack, "Le mystere Jeanne Calment," Sept a Huit, TF1, March 2019. [Online]. Available: https://rutube.ru/video/ f77fddb53878337d110569b7280459a6/? fbclid=IwAR2QlT_9s0_HPMbKGbKhL-Y3S_bgwzM2zyMOFLo2YTkpJMTI4UBbzuh6Dm 8.

[84] R. Baheux, "Affaire Jeanne Calment : «Si c'était sa fille, c'était une menteuse exceptionnelle»," Le Parisien, January 2019. [Online]. Available: https://www.leparisien.fr/ societe/affaire-jeanne-calment-si-c-etait-sa-fille-c-etait-une-menteuse-exceptionnelle-25-01-2019-7996386.php.

[85] J.-M. Morandini, "Heritages NRJ 12 : Spéciale Jeanne Calment," Carson TV, 2019. [Online]. Available: https://www.youtube.com/watch? v=6jmicEYqj3g.

[86] R. Baheux, "Age de Jeanne Calment : l'Etat a-t-il

«fermé les yeux»?," Le Parisien, December 2018. [Online]. Available: https://www.leparisien.fr/ societe/age-de-jeanne-calment-l-etat-a-t-il- ferme-les-yeux-31-12-2018-7978791.php.

[87]   M. Allard, "Dimension sociétale du phénomène jeanne-calment: mythe moderne?," vol. 43, no. 3, pp. 27-40, 2021.

[88]   M.-S. Lorner, "120 ans, le bon Dieu a dû m'oublier," *VSD*, January 1995.

[89]   C. Levraud, "Dissertation for the competency of gerontology: Jeanne Calment 118 years, a longevity precedent," University Library of Medicine of Marseille, 1993. [Online].

[90]   G. Garoyan, "Cent-quatorze ans de vie ou la longue histoire de Jeanne Calment," Université d'Aix-Marseille, 1990.

[91]   Y. Christen, "Cent vingt ans - ma journee avec Jeanne, la doyenne du monde," Le Figaro, 1995.

[92]   N. McWhirter and G. Walters, "Next week she will be the oldest person ever," *The Times*, 14 Oct 1995.

[93]   C. W. Fetrow and J. R. Avila, "The Complete Guide to Herbal Medicines," p. 112, 2000.

[94]   S. B. Herter, "No More Tiaras: (A Memoir of Eight Decades)," p. 147.

[95]   C. Buchard, "L'adieu au siecle de Jeanne," *Paris Match*, no. 2516, p. 90, Aug 1997.

[96]   A. Sage, "Six score and one. She saw the Eiffel tower to go up and already was a pensioner when Hitler invaded France. Adam Sage meets the oldest human being in history," *The Observer* , 18 Feb 1996.

ANNEX: TIMELINE

Unknown date	Jacob pretends to be his brother Esau to get his father's blessing
104 BCE	Romans build a canal from Arles to Marseille
50 BCE	Arles supports Caesar against Pompey
6-2 BCE	Jesus Christ is born
29-34	Jesus Christ dies (or not)
70	Destruction of the Jewish state by the Romans
245	Pope Fabian sent out Trophimus to Arles to teach the Gospel
312	Constantin the Great converts to Christianity
313	The assembly of Christian bishops in the Western Roman Empire meets in Arles
917	French King Charles the Simple invites Kalonymos family to France

X century	The tower of the Porcelet castle in Arles is built. It is still present in Maison Calment
XI-XII	Modern structure of St. Trophime cathedral built in Arles
XII century	Kalonymos I the Great from the house of David ruled the Jewish kingdom of Narbonne for around sixty years and lived to be ninety years of age
1286	A famous Jewish satirist, Kalonymos ben Kalonymos ben Meir born in Arles
XIII century	The castle in Pouzilhac transferred to the house of Uzès from King Philip IV
1297	The Jews of Uzès accused of ritual murder
1306	King Philip IV expels the Jews from France
1348	Black death devastates Provence
1394	Charles VI "the madman" expels Jews from France
XV century	Garin Calmenc – the oldest known ancestor, 12 generations before Jeanne, lives in Pouzilhac while Isaac Nathan ben Kalonymos lives in Arles
1481	Acquisition of Provence by France
May 10,	Arles Synagogue is destroyed

1484	
1493	Remaining Jews expelled from Provence
1627	Gaillard Calmen born in Pouzilhac 7 generations before Jeanne
1670	Gaillard relocates from Pouzilhac to Arles after being attacked and robbed of his mules
1720	Black death in Arles kills 25% of the population
1723	Vincent Calmen (first carpenter in the dynasty) born in Arles 4 generations before Jeanne
1788	Pierre Calment Jeanne's great-grandfather (first ship carpenter in the dynasty) marries Marthe Fréou,
July 14 1789	Storming of the Bastille
1837	Cholera outbreak
1837	Nicolas Calment is born
16 Oct 1861	Nicolas Calment and Marguerite Gilles married
1862	Their son Antoine is born (died age 4)
1863	Their daughter Marie is born (died in infancy)
1865	Cholera outbreak

25 Apr 1865	Jeanne Calment's brother François Calment is born
23 Dec 1867	Piano teacher Césarie Gachon is born
16 Jan 1868	Jacques Calment and Maria Félix married
2 Nov 1868	Fernand Calment is born
1870	France loses the war to Bismarck's Prussia, the Second French empire collapses and the Third Respublic is declared

21 Feb 1875	Jeanne Calment is born at 5 rue du Roure
1875	First permanent Trinquetaille bridge opened
1878	Emile Fassin becomes Mayor of Arles
1880	Madame Benet opens her school at the rue de la Calade
1881	Nicolas Calment builds multiple barges (penelles) for the company "Alais sur Rhône"
28 Mar 1882	State education becomes secular and mandatory for boys and girls
1883	rue Gambetta is built
1883	Madame Meyffren takes over Madame Benet

	in her school
Jul 1884	Arles cholera outbreak
1884	Jacques buys back part of the building at rue Gambetta at the candle auction
1885	Nicolas Calment sells the barges after the bankruptcy of the railway company
1885	Jean Baptiste Calment, partner of Nicolas, dies
1885	Marthe Fousson is born in Fontvieille
1885	Jeanne's family moves to 53 rue de la Roquette
20 Oct 1885	Reopening for Jacques Calment's Grands Magasins de Nouveautes
13 May 1886	Jacques Calment dies of typhoid fever
1886	Fernand gets baccalaureate in the College of Arles
1886	Madame Benet reopens her school
1886	Girls' secondary courses open in Arles at rue St. Paul
28 Jan 1887	Eiffel Tower construction started

20 Feb 1888	Vincent Van Gogh arrives in Arles
23 Dec 1888	Van Gogh severs his ear
1888	Jeanne's father bought a farm Rouiron in St. Martin de Crau
1888	Fernand is free from army service as the only son of a widow. He is a trader in Arles.
31 Mar 1889	Eiffel Tower completed in Paris
1889	Madame Benet closes her school
1889	Secondary courses move from rue St. Paul to rue du Cloître
8 May 1889	Van Gogh goes to St. Remy asylum
27 Jul 1890	Death of Van Gogh
1890	Fernand gets a shooting prize during celebrations in Arles
1890	Marriage of François Calment and Marguerite Olympe Bouquet in Toulon
1891	Fernand, member of velo club of Arles finishes at 10th place at the 5km race

1891	Jeanne gets 11 nominations as a second-year student in secondary courses for girls
5 Mar 1891	Jeanne Calment's future son-in-law Joseph Billot is born
1892	Fernand is Commissaire at the music club Estudiantina
Dec 1894	Dreyfus convicted of treason
1894	Espartero killed by a bull in Madrid
1895	The barge with coal La Jeanne owned by Bizalion ran aground in Arles
May 1895	Fernand on vacation in Hotel des Alpes, Uriage-les-Bains
1896	Fernand fights with thieves in Maison Calment using a revolver

8 Apr 1896	Marriage of Fernand Calment and Jeanne Calment
1896	Jeanne's niece, Marie Calment born in Toulon
4 Oct 1896	Espartero fatally wounded at bullfight in Nimes
1897	Fernand is Commissaire of the committee in Association of former students at College of Arles (AFSCA)

1897	Painter and sculptor Claude Férigoule and his wife relocate to Arles from Avignon
1897	Maison Calment starts selling furniture
20 Jan 1898	Jeanne Calment's daughter Yvonne Calment born
14 Apr 1898	Jeanne attends the marriage of Marius Deshons and Marguerite Crouanson in Marseille
5 Jun 1900	Jeanne attends Marriage of Louis Vial and Marthe Calment
1900	Honoré Nicolas becomes mayor of Arles
1901	Fernand and his cousins Nicolas Crouanson and Louis Calment participate in organization of Grand Bal Mireille in Arles
1901	Jeanne and Fernand on vacation in Hotel du Midi, Uriage-les-Bains, Maria also there
1902	Fernand on vacation in Hotel du Midi, Uriage-les-Bains
1902	Boudignion launches a mahonne for the port of Marseille
1903	Fernand becomes member in Friends of old Arles
1903	Joseph Billot gets certificate of education in private congregational school, rue d'Amphitheatre

~1903	Jeanne paints the paravent
1903	Jeanne and Yvonne on vacation in Hotel du Midi, Uriage-les-Baines
1904	Calments become shareholders of the Cercle d'Avenir
July 1904	Calments attend baptism of Germaine Fassin
20 Aug 1904	Fernand with Jeanne on vacation in Aix-les-Bains
10 Dec 1904	Mistral awarded the Nobel Prize in literature
16 Jan 1905	Nicolas Calment resigns as administrator of benefits office after a scandal
1905	Town crosses removed by mayor as an act against religion
9 Dec 1905	Separation of church and state in France. Religious schools close
1905	Joseph Billot gets a third prize at boys drawing school directed by Férigoule
1905	Jeanne donates to widows of soldiers killed in Russo-Japanese war
1905-1906	Yvonne participates in group photos in the school yard at Secondary courses for girls in

	Arles, rue du Cloître
1906	The cook Marthe Fousson lives with Calments and accompanies Yvonne to school
1906	Dreyfus exonerated
1906	A fire devastates Maison Mareau, a big neighbouring store on the place Antonelle, Claude Calment was the chief firefighter but couldn't help
8 Dec 1906	Mathieu Félix dies and leaves his daughters (including Yvonne's grandmother Maria Félix) "Mas de Prentegarde" on the Rhône near Arles. Yvonne bathes in Rhône and catches cold there. Jeanne thinks this was the cause of her disease

1907	On the place of the burnt store the new huge Nouvelle Galleries store is built by Maube brothers. It would outcompete both Calment and Bouisson stores and is still there
1907	Fernand becomes a vice-president of Gallic hunting society
1907	Jeanne is an advisor in society of mutual help for workers in Arles
1907	Maria retires, reorganization and renaming of the store to Maison Fernand Calment
10 May	Jean Granaud becomes Mayor of Arles

1908	
1908	Jeanne and Fernand on vacation in Hotel du Midi, Uriage-les-Baines
1908	Jules Dallard rents Enclos Rouabaud (Salle des fetes) at Bld. des Lices for the Folies Arlésiennes
1909	Fernand participates in the banquet for former students of Lycée of Avignon
1909	A school opens in Archbishop palace adjacent to St. Trophime
1909	Boudignion launches a mahonne in Arles
1909	François exhibits his painting "l'Effet de Mistral au Brusc" in "Le salon Toulonnais"
May 1909	Unveiling of Mistral's statue
June 1910	Yvonne gets certificate d'etudes primaire
Jul 1910	Yvonne attends Secondary courses for girls in Arles with Nevière, granddaughter of midwife who helped her to be born
1911	Fernand is vice-president in AFSCA
1911	A boat "Madeleine" was stolen from Honoré Boudignion's shipyard in Arles
1912	Jeanne donates for the construction of a military aircraft "Frédéric Mistral" through Escolo Mistralenco

1912	Pierre Fassin, grandson of Emile born
1913	Fernand on vacation in Aix-les-Bains without Jeanne
25 Mar 1914	Frédéric Mistral dies
1913	Fernand on vacation in Aix-les-Bains
1914	Fernand, Jeanne, and Yvonne on vacation in Hotel du Midi, Uriage-les-Bains
July 1914	Dr. Urpar organizes the costume festival in Arles
28 Jul 1914	Outbreak of World War One
1914	Fernand is mobilized but is not sent to the front
1914	Shooting and military preparation society organizes a concert in Maison Calment
1914	Fernand is an editor of "Tra Provenclando", a brochure devoted to promotion of Esperanto
1914	Jeanne is a member in Union of Women of France (Red cross). She makes donations for feeding soldiers at the station
1915	Jeanne member of the "Soldier's kitchen"
1915	Dr. Urpar dies
1915	Dr. Louis Rey opens antituberculosis

	dispenser in Arles
1914 -192 5	Fernand is a member of patronage committee for primary superior school in Arles
1915	Fernand is collecting donations for the Committee for national defence
1916	Fernand is collecting donations for Anti-German society of Arles
Aug 1916	Jeanne Calment at spa in Savoy
1916	Piano teacher Césarie Gachon dies
1916 -191 7	Joseph's courage is mentioned in his military file
1917	Jeanne's niece, Marie Calment dies in Toulon

11 Nov 1918	Armistice of World War One
16 Mar 1919	Doctor Joseph Morizot becomes Mayor of Arles
8 Oct 1919	wedding of Countess de Divonne marquis de Forton
25 Nov 1921	Joseph deployed in Syria
May	Millerand visits Arles, his driver looks like

1922	Joseph Billot
28 Dec 1922	Joseph on leave
19 Jan 1923	Joseph takes up duties in Morocco
29 May 1922	Emile Fassin dies
1922	Van Gogh biographer Coquiot visits Arles and asks Doctor Félix Rey to connect him with those who had met Van Gogh
30 Jun 1923	Yvonne attends the Costume festival in Arles. Joseph and Nenette Billot seen in Peugeot
1923	Jeanne's photo is taken by photographer Ouvière; it will later be used on her ID card
18 Sep 1924	Jeanne Calment's mother Marguerite Gilles dies
11 July 1925	Joseph on 4 months leave
1 Dec 1925	Joseph resident in Fontainbleau
20 Jan 1926	Frédéric Billot's wife Renée Taque born
4 Feb 1926	Yvonne Calment and Joseph Billot marry and go to Fontainebleau, quartier Lariboisiere
15 Mar	Nicolas donates his property to his

1926	children, Jeanne, and François
June 1926	Yvonne and Joseph attent the wedding of Antoinette Billot and Pierre Flauder
July 1926	Yvonne is seen in the list of 1000FF bond lottery winners
9 Aug 1926	Joseph in Toul, automotive equipment depot
Sep 27 1926	Launch of sanatorium for tuberculous patients in Passy-Praz-Coutant, Haute-Savoie
Nov 1926	Maria and Jeanne seen at Mass for Beatification of Jean Marie du Lau
23 Dec 1926	Jeanne Calment's grandson Frédéric Billot born
9 Jan 1927	Baptism for Freddy Billot
1927	Fernand is president of Commission of Corso (organization of the parade in Arles)
Apr 1927	A nurse in the group photo after exam in hospital in Arles looks like Yvonne but is probably Jeanne
7 Oct 1927	Joseph in Smithies Inspection, Paris
1927	De la Faille validates Wacker's Self-portrait at Easel
1928	Calments buy neighbouring property from

	the Boudignion-Coron couple to establish a furniture store there
10 Jun 1928	Joseph Billot granted leave from Army for five years, due to Yvonne's health
1928	Yvonne treated in *Haute Savoie*
January 1929	Arnaud, Feuillas, Silvestre get medal for their service in Maison Calment
May 1929	Yvonne and Joseph Billot photographed at wedding of Jean Paul Billot

29 Oct 1929	Wall Street crash
1928, 1930	Fernand is Committee member in celebrations in Arles
1930	Celebration of Mistral Centenary. Fernand is commissaire of Corso, participates in flowered automobiles registration
1930	Yvonne seen in traditional costume in Arles
31 Aug 1930	Paul Fassin (son of Emile and father of Pierre) dies from stroke while hunting
1930	Sanatorium Hotel Belvédère reopens in Leysin
22 Jan 1931	Jeanne Calment's father Nicolas Calment dies
11 Apr	Jeanne Calment's mother-in-law Maria

1931	Calment dies
19 Jun	Fernand and Jeanne sell mas St. Jacques
Jul 1931	Yvonne with l'Escolo Mistralenco in Arles
24 Jul 1931	Fernand sells a café in Arles on behalf of François
Aug 1931	Yvonne Calment photographed in Hotel Belvédère, Leysin. The last picture of Jeanne and Yvonne together is also taken there. Jeanne suffers from tuberculosis and is treated by Dr. Maurice Gilbert
1931	A famous pianist Jacqueline Blancard (wife of Dr. Miege) plays piano in Belvédère
19 Sept 1931	Fernand takes part in music festival (manifestation in honour of Fernand Beissier) without Jeanne
28 Nov 1931	Jeanne sells house at 53 rue de la Roquette
1932	Boudignion launches a mahonne in Arles
1932	Employee of Maison Calment, Marius Maxence gets a gold medal for his work
Feb 1932	Jeanne signs use of funds
Dec 1932	Doctor Maurice Gilbert marries his patient Paulette Kellner
Dec	Fernand delivers a speech in honour of Dr.

1932	Félix Rey after his death earlier this year
6 Apr 1932	Otto Wacker trial for Van Gogh forgeries
May 1932	Joseph on drill
1932	Fernand quits position of the Vice-president of Cercle d'Avenir
21 May 1932	Noë Masson becomes mayor of Arles
24 Jun 1932	Notary Arnaud retires, David takes over
17 Sep 1932	Death of Dr. Félix Rey
Dec 1932	Fernand as president of the Association of Former Students of the College of Arles, dedicates a speech in memory of Dr. Félix Rey after his death earlier that year
11 Jan 1933	Jeanne's ID card registered with changed signature
30 Jan 1933	Adolph Hitler appointed as Chancellor of Germany
16 Feb 1933	Jeanne buys villa in Paradou with changed signature
10 Jun 1933	Joseph Billot renews his army leave for another five years
8 Jan 1934	Alexandre Stavisky killed

13 Jan 1934	Funeral for Jerome Arnaud, employee of the store

19 Jan 1934	Death of Jeanne/Yvonne Calment
20 Jan 1934	Funeral for Yvonne Calment
6 Feb 1934	Political riots in Paris
Mar 1934	Jean Granaud dies, the whole town attends the funeral
July-Sept 1934	Fernand alone in Uriage
1934	Anatole Sixte-Quenin becomes Mayor of Arles for SFIO
1935	Dr. Gilbert and Dr. Miege publish the results of gold sault treatment of 100 patients in the Hotel Belvédère, Leysin
1935	François paints the sea
11 Nov 1935	Sudden death of Joseph Morizot at a banquet of former combatants
1935	Fernand takes a 150000FF loan from a bank backed by Maison Calment

1935	Fernand participates in donations for needy elderly
21 Jun 1936	Joseph Imbert elected Mayor of Arles for SFIO
1937	Calments sell their property in St. Marie de la Mer
1937	Billot family reunion in Paris. Madame Calment visits Versailles with Freddy and Robert Billot
1938	Maison Calment closes
1 April 1938	Joseph returns to army duties
1938	Fernand participates in AFSCA Excursion to aviation camp in Istres with Férigoule
19 Jan 1939	Jeanne's sister-in-law Marguerite Olympe Bouquet dies in Toulon
1939	Fernand participates in the AFSCA campaign of stamps against tuberculosis
1 Sep 1939	Outbreak of World War Two
18 June 1940	Joseph Billot, a commandant in 4th group of 112 R.A.L. passes orders to defenders of Maginot line at Epinal
Jun 1941	A man similar to Joseph seen with general

	Dentz for Vichy French in Syria
July 14 1941	French army of Levant forces surrender in Syria
Sept 1941	Joseph in charge of helping soldiers returning from Syria in Marseille
Oct 1941	Joseph Billot returns to Arles after being prisoner of war. His return is celebrated in *Cercle d'Avenir*. Joseph asks people to collaborate with Pétain
6 Jan 1942	Mistral's bronze statue is removed as scrap for the German war effort
20 Aug 1942	Joseph Billot awarded Officer Legion of Honour by general Dentz
2 Oct 1942	Jeanne Calment's husband Fernand Calment dies from liver disease after cherry poisoning. His will is to leave everything to his grandson
Nov 1942	Germans occupy Arles
2 Mar 1943	Joseph Imbert arrested by Germans for resistance activities
1943	Madame Calment pictured with her hunting dog in Paradou
1943	Freddy buys half of the Rouiron farm from François

1944	Joseph Billot is elected administrator of the Arlesian branch of the Bouche du Rhône Savings Bank
25 Jun 1944	Van Gogh's yellow house destroyed by bombs
6 Aug 1944	Railway bridge in Arles destroyed
15 Aug 1944	Trinquetaille bridge destroyed by bombs
24 Aug 1944	Liberation of Arles
October 1944	Joseph is major of the Ammunition General Stock Warehouse in Miramas
8 Jan 1945	Death of Joseph Imbert in German prisoner camp

2 Sep 1945	End of World War Two
Dec 1945	General Dentz dies in prison
1946	Calments pay the War tax
3 Mar 1950	Frédéric Billot's and Renée Taque marry
1951	Madame Calment and Freddy sell the family

	farm Rouiron
1954	Freddy dedicates his medical thesis
1955	Freddy leaves a will to pass everything to his wife in the case of his death
10 Dec 1962	Jeanne Calment's brother François Calment dies in hospice de Chiavary in Arles
25 Jan 1963	Jeanne Calment's son-in-law Joseph Billot dies
13 Aug 1963	Jeanne Calment's grandson Frédéric Billot dies in car accident
1963	Unfair deal between Renée Taque and Jeanne Calment
1964	Taque passes the viager to CNP
13 Aug 1964	Mme Calment disputes the deal with Taque in the court in Tarascon
1967	Dispute over en viager and property sales resolves in favour of Calment, the rent is increased and she gets her villa La Miquelette in Paradou back
1968	Mme Calment sells the villa in Paradou
1968	Taque had no money to repay the debt, so she had taken several loans backed by her property in Maison Calment and asked her notary Raffray to divide this property into

	22 lots to sell them separately
1969	Raffray takes over the viager deal
1972	Taque remarries, Raffray is a witness
21 Feb 1975	Mme Calment's 100th birthday, she visits communist mayor Jacques Perrot
1980	Dr Maurice Gilbert dies after telling his children he had treated Jeanne Calment
1980	Mme Calment meets Lucien de Cock at the stairs of St. Trophime
1982	Raffray divorces and now his first wife must pay part of the rent to Calment
1985	Mme Calment moves into the Maison du Lac and orders Josette Bigonnet to destroy her archives
1985	Raffray buys more property from Taque
1986	Earliest reports of Calment meeting Van Gogh
21 Feb 1986	The oldest man Shigechiyo Izumi dies at validated age of 120 years (later debunked)
21 Oct 1986	Augusta Holtz dies at the validated age of 115 years 79 days – the oldest validated B47supercentenarian among those born before Jeanne Calment
1988	Mme Calment becomes longevity record

	holder
1988	Paris Match interview with Mme Calment
1989	Calment appears in film Vincent and Me
1990	Taque sells an apartment on the third floor of Maison Calment to Chico Bouchikhi from the music group Gipsy King
1990	Mme Calment hospitalised after fall

Jun 1992	Validators start recording interviews
Feb 1883	Mme Calment is introduced to Emile Laurent
Sep 1994	Final interviews for book
Nov 1994	Validators complete Jeanne Calment book (French version)
1995	Demographer Nicolas Brouard publicly suggests the possibility of identity switch
Feb 1995	The international team of experts including Bernard Jeune and James Vaupel visits and validates Mme Calment
25 Dec 1995	Raffray dies
19 Feb	Mme Calment releases rap CD

1996	
Fen 1996	Paris Match bring Mme Calment her piano
1996	Mme Calment is isolated from journalists and validators
4 Aug 1997	Mme Calment death is followed by quick funeral without autopsy
1999	Tom Kirkwood mentions the possibility of identity switch but suggests « we should banish such thoughts from our minds »
30 Dec 1999	Sarah Knauss dies at validated age of 119 years and 97 days without birth record available
2002	The « International Database of Longevity » launched by Robine and Vaupel
2003	Antoinette Billot dies age 100
2006	Jacques de Baudus publishes his article on the Calment's identity switch without any reaction
2011	James Vaupel suggests that most people born since the year 2000 will probably become centenarians
2012	Nicolas Brouard reiterates his concerns in a conference poster
2016	Julliette Espeyte dies age 102
Oct	Zak blocked from the 110club forum for

2018	raising concerns about the longevity record
Nov 2018	Zak's paper « Negligent senescence or life annuity » in the Proceedings of the Gerontology Section of the Moscow Society of Naturalists (in Russian)
4 Dec 2018	Valery Novoselov gives interview about the switch to Lifespan.io
Dec 2018	Yury Deigin publishes his review of the switch hypothesis on Habr, Medium and Twitter
19 Dec 2018	Zak publishes a paper « Jeanne Calment: the Secret of Longevity » on *Researchgate*
31 Dec 2018	AFP distributes the report about the switch
Jan 2019	Facebook counter-investigation group is launched by Arlesians
Jan 2019	The Washington Post publishes an article about « The Russian Conspiracy Theory »
30 Jan 2019	Rejuvenation Research journal edited by Aubrey de Grey publishes Zak's paper
May 2019	Zak and Gibbs publish « Bayesian Assessment of the Longevity of Jeanne Calment » on *Researchgate*
Sep 2019	The paper "The Real Facts Supporting Jeanne Calment as the Oldest Ever Human"

	published by Robine, Allard, Jeune and Hermann calls for retraction of Zak's paper
11 Mar 2020	Renée Taque dies
Feb 2020	Rejuvenation Research publishes several papers for and against the switch
2021	The book « Exceptional Lifespans » by Max Planck Institute for Demographic Research reaffirms Calment's longevity record
Apr 2021	Gibbs and Zak publish « A Review of Longevity Validations to 2020 »
27 Mar 2022	James Vaupel dies
6 Apr 2022	Kane Tanaka surpasses the age of Sarah Knauss
19 Apr 2022	Kane Tanaka dies
Aug 2022	Mme Calment on the main page of the Bouches-du-Rhône archives website

Printed in Great Britain
by Amazon

42675870R00116